Exotic

MW00777621

Society, Culture, Hospitality & Traditions

Revised Extended Edition
178 TESTED RECIPES
WITH FOOD COMPOSITION TABLES

Compiled and edited

by
Daniel J. Mesfin

Published by Ethiopian Cookbook Enterprises
of Falls Church, VA
3800 Powell Lane, Suite 404
Falls Church, VA 22041

i

Ethiopian Cookbook Enterprises
3800 Powell Lane #404
Falls Church, VA 22041

Library of Congress Catalog Card Number: 89–081056

Printed in the United States of America.

Photographs by: *E. Tesfa, photographer, Washington, DC*
T. Fisseha, photographer, VA

*Back Cover Photo compliments of BLUE NILE RESTAURANT, 103 W. 77th St. at
Columbus Ave., New York City, (212) 580-3232. At the BLUE NILE delicious
Ethiopian home cooking is served on an authentic "MESOB," a straw
basket-table with three-legged wood stool. Ethiopian beauty is wearing national
dress of embroidered cotton.*

*Front Cover (KITFO/STEAK TARTAR p.116) Photo compliments of Meskerem
Restaurant, 2434 18th St. NW, Washington, D.C. (202) 462-4100. One of the
finest and most spacious Ethiopian restaurants in North America with its
traditional decor designed by a renowned Ethiopian artist. Meskerem was
selected by Esquire magazine (November 1985) as one of the outstanding
restaurants in North America.*

Dedication

This Ethiopian cookbook is dedicated in particular to my mother, Weiyzero YeshiEmebet Guma, and to all Ethiopian mothers and to all those humanitarians who have helped Ethiopia and her people in time of dire need.

Daniel Jote Mesfin

EMAMA TSIGE

Immense contribution in the making of this book.

Acknowledgements

This volume, covering a broad spectrum of recipes, is published in collaboration with specialists, who have checked the material pertaining to their fields and contributed relevant information.
Acknowledgements are due to the following:

Mrs. Adwa Abayneh
Weiyzerit* Seble Adam
Weiyzero** Guenet Alemu
Mr. Shlomo Bachrach
Dr. Esther Balogh
(microbiologist)
Prof. Z. Boszormenyi
(biochemist)
Mrs. Polly Damamn
Mrs. Marian Duneas
Mrs. Joy Evans
Mr. Theodros Fissha
Weizero Debritu Gessesse
Weiyzero Menbere Haile
Giorgis
Weiyzero Afomia Haile
Mariam
Mr. Richard R. Herbert
Weiyzero Ketsela Kebede
Weiyzero Derejash Work
Kitaw
Dr. Alyce S. Klussman
Mrs. Truwork Kidane Mariam
Weiyzerit Tsehay Kidane
Mariam

Ato*** Wolde Kidane
Mariam
Mrs. Helen Lamb
Mrs. Marilyn Larsen
Weiyzero Rahel Mesfin
Mrs. Sheron Metevia
Mrs. Maureen McWalters
Weiyzero Saba I. Mekbib
Miss Nancy Park
Mrs. Susan Park
Mr. Lou Rou
Mrs. Polly Scoville
Miss Rebecca Scoville
Mr. Russel Scoville
Weiyzero Asegedech
Sebsebe
Weiyzero Tsige Seleshi
Weiyzero Tsige Sharew
Weiyzero Emena Sheferaw
Mrs. Joyce Sutherland
Ato Dawit Teklu
Weiyzero Fekerte Teklu
Mr. John L. Withers
Weiyzero Leah Workneh
Tedros

Special thanks to Weiyzero Afomia Haile Mariam, Weiyzerit Tsehay Kidane Mariam, Weiyzero Tsige Seleshi, Weiyzero Fekerte Teklu, and to all those Ethiopians and their families who researched, tested, evaluated and provided invaluable assistance.

Acknowledgements

Special thanks also go to Dr. Alyce Klussman who prepared the format for the recipes and performed the first edit of original recipe drafts and Ato Alem Mezgebe for giving the final look to the book and for transliterating Ethiopian names and words.

Special thanks to Prof. Z. Boszormenyi and Dr. Esther Balogh presently working in the dept of Science and Technology of Food Institute of Ecology Awolowo Univ of IFE ILE-IFE, NIGERIA for the valuable assistance in their contribution.

Weiyzerit Miss
**Weiyzero Mrs
***Ato—Mr

Contents

Exotic Ethiopian Cooking

Contents

Contents

Contents

Contents

Preface

by
Daniel Jote Mesfin

This cookbook is by no means exhaustive. But I hope it will offer a taste of Ethiopia and give a true meaning to the adage "variety is the spice of life" by virtue of its cultural diversity.

Being ancient may not be a qualification *per se* or even flattering at times, but in Ethiopia's case it is. Longevity and continuity of values have produced a unique cultural pattern and an enigmatic mentality that have not ceased to fascinate and intrigue the most intrepid observers since time immemorial.

Gibbon's contention that the "Abyssinians slept a thousand years forgetful of the world by whom they were forgotten" does not hold water since our introversion did much to develop a personality all our own. And the geography—our mountain fastness and the hostile lowlands—which Gibbons scorned for our millenia of slumber thankfully acted as the concrete that strengthened that personality. It also determined our history and lifestyle.

The world's major religions—Judaism, Christianity and Islam—homed in on the mystery that was Ethiopia. They blended to form a cultural pattern unparalleled anywhere in a manner that literally projects a reflection of the social and religious history of the ancient world. Hence, our strict observance of their taboos in our dietary habits. Reason why you will find nowhere in this book any recipe for a pork dish. You will discover, however, a rich variety of vegetarian recipes—all our women's pride and diners' delight.

Our culinary art and food habits make a delicious part of our cultural mosaic in the same way our traditional costumes manifest that culture in a rhapsody of colors. Their significance goes beyond the chore of cooking and the routine of eating. So much so that they have attained artistic heights and created their own value judgement.

Cooking demands unbridled imagination as eating commands a delicate style. Unlike the Western individual table manners, ours reflect our communal dining traditions. People eat from a common platter and the pace of taking in food is more or less uniform. Even a hungry stomach respects the speed limit. And though food is eaten with the hand—the right hand—licking one's fingers is frowned upon.

Feeding a guest by placing big chunks of food into his or her mouth is a mark of honor or affection. This is done with the accompanying remark that feeding just once causes a rift, twice endears, the third time round leads to argument.

Although this sounds quaint, it is symbolic. If you feed your guest once and don't do it again, you are acting the miser. The recipient does not argue. The second time, he or she says that is enough. The hostess insists. The third time the guest and hostess insist. Don't ever imagine meal time is fighting time. On the contrary, it is a game. The hostess must display her hospitality at all times. And the guest must never act like a glutton or one who has nothing to eat at home.

An Ethiopian man is always the diner; never the cook. The kitchen is off-limits to him. His woman doubles up as cook, servant and waitress. In a childless household, she washes her husband's feet and brings him a vessel and water pot for him to wash his hand before touching food. Washing hands before a meal is a must. The lady of the house only promotes herself to chef if she can afford domestic help or has a daughter.

A woman worth her salt values her cooking no less than her looks. In fact, she is more partial to her cooking because she is socially judged by it: an unaccomplished woman makes her husband a laughing stock. Her honor, therefore, depends on her standing in society. It is also a matter of honor and duty that she creates her daughter in her own image—a good cook, housewife and mother. That attribute and her virginity make her a prize catch for a suitor. In this catalogue of virtues, good conduct, pleasant character and respectability are plus points. For, as our saying goes, a good wife is her husband's crown.

Preface

It is such women who invented these recipes that made Ethiopian cooking distinctive. But you must be forwarned that cooking is individual. No two women—even mother and daughter—never cook a dish the same way. For it is done by instinct. This book has provided measurements to make your venture easy. With time, you will learn to cook by instinct, too. That is when you will occupy a place of distinction among Ethiopian women regardless of your nationality, race or creed. And to bring you to that goal we have transliterated Ethiopian names and words as near to the way we pronounce them as possible.

This is your baptism of fire. Surprise your family or friends with no further ado. Feast them with dishes some of which date back to the time of the Queen of Sheba.

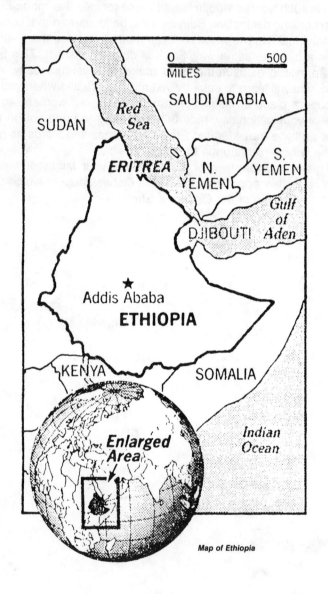

Map of Ethiopia

Introduction

Ethiopian food is like the Ethiopians themselves: spicy, subtle, piquant and most of all, unforgettable.

The variety is astonishing. Are you a vegetarian? So are millions of Coptic Christian Ethiopians, for some 200 days a year. To meet the need, their ancient culture produced and refined scores of vegetarian dishes with great delicacy of flavorings. Are you a carnivore? An Ethiopian meal might lead you to think you were already in heaven. Beef cooked and beef raw, beef cubed and beef ground, beef marinated in a fiery red pepper sauce with more flavors blended in than the most sophisticated foreign palate can identify, beef stewed in a sauce that can make you sweat or make you sing, or both. And lamb. And goat. But no pork, which is avoided by both Ethiopian Moslems and Christians.

And of course chicken, too, is probably the most widely known Ethiopian dish of all: *doro we't* (chicken in sauce). A festive meal without a richly flavored *doro we't*, and a hardboiled egg or two steeped in that extraordinary *we't* is practically a contradiction in terms. And complementing the vital flavors of the *we't* with its red pepper base and its original (every cook has her secrets) blend of spices and herbs, is the slightly sour *injera*, a pancake crepe that is eaten even as it serves as fork, spoon and knife. The contrast between the spicy *we't* and the sensible *injera* is high culinary art.

Why is Ethiopian food so delicious? And if it really is so, why isn't it better known?

To talk about Ethiopian cuisine, it is necessary to talk about Ethiopia. Except during tragic droughts, such as the past twelve years—the highlands of Ethiopia receive a heavy rainfall—so heavy, in fact that since the dawn of time the Nile has been overflowing in Egypt, thousands of miles away, with the runoff from the well-soaked highlands.

The normally plentiful rainfall, and the wonderfully temperate climate of those plateaus so near the equator but over a mile high, have always been hospitable to growing things, plant and animal. Cattle, sheep and goats have thrived for thousands of years beyond the reach of the tse-tse and other tropical scourges. Grains and vegetables ripen after every rainy season. Sometimes there are Small Rains as well as Big Rains, and then the earth is even more bountiful.

Although most Ethiopians live on the plateau where the air sparkles and braces, there are mountains to 15,000 feet and deserts below sea level, and a river gorge that can swallow up the entire Grand Canyon (deeper *and* wider). The variety of plants that grow in these habitats, and the zones in between, is so great that Ethiopia is recognized as one of the few remaining treasure houses of plant genes in the world. Thousands of years ago, the Ethiopians realized that they lived in one of Nature's finest spice gardens. Seizing the opportunity, they invented, and have steadily perfected, the blends of spices that linger in the mind long after they have faded from the tongue.

A favored climate and Nature's bounty partly explain the richness of Ethiopia's cuisine. But another ingredient is the time— not just a century or two, but ten, fifteen, even twenty centuries—required for traditions to mature, to absorb the influences of neighboring cultures across the surrounding Red Sea and desert barriers, while remaining unquestionably Ethiopian. Regional variations reflect local crops and other influences, but over the centuries a national cuisine has emerged.

Why has Ethiopian cooking remained a well-kept secret? Perhaps it is because Ethiopia, the Abyssinia of earlier times, has had so little contact with any but its neighbors. Marco Polo never visited (though Vasco de Gama's son did, and is buried there). Perhaps it is because most of Ethiopia was never colonized, merely occupied by the Italian fascists for a few years, and so was never brought into intimate relations with a world power. Perhaps it is because nowhere else could one find a matching natural spice shelf, or the favored grain (*t'ef*) for the *injera*, which grows best at high elevations.

Introduction

Even now, it is the Ethiopians themselves, who wouldn't dream of leaving their cooking behind, who are bringing it to us. In cities across the United States, Ethiopian restaurants now serve the growing numbers of refugees who have escaped a brutal and dogmatic regime. The few Americans who have been to Ethiopia can't believe their good luck when an Ethiopian restaurant opens nearby. A few adventurous others wander in, intrigued. A few more are brought by Ethiopian friends. And so it grows. Once hooked, it's for life.

Much more could be written. About a cuisine that developed completely without sugar, and that traditionally put salt in its coffee. About a country where coffee trees still grow wild, and where they probably grew first in a province called Kefa. About a country where feeding one's guests is taken literally: a host or hostess will take a piece of *injera*, wrap it around the choicest morsels and put the whole parcel, a care package if ever there was one, into the guest's mouth.

But all this would put off the feast, and we've waited too long already. So turn the page, find your favorites in the table of contents, and get busy.

Shlomo-Bachrach

Society, Culture, Hospitality, and Traditions in Ethiopia

A country of majestic mountains and deserts with lunar landscape, Ethiopia is a metaphor of diversity. An embodiment of geographical and climatic contrasts, a mosaic of peoples, and a repository of distinct cultural strands, it also offers a catalogue of flora and fauna of extraordinary variety some of which are endemic to the country.

Variously called the "Roof of Africa," a country of "Perennial Spring," "Land of 13 months of Sunshine," and, historically, "Land of Prester John," even "the Breadbasket of the Middle East," Ethiopia borders on Utopia. Although not quite Sir Thomas Moore's fictional idyllic place (concocted from Greek words "ou" meaning not and "topos" meaning a place,) immortalized in his 1516 book of the same name, these co-instantaneous facts taken together, nevertheless, literally cast a picture of exotic beauty of the country with a touch of mystery about its people.

With a plateau of panoramic view rising to 8,000 feet surrounded almost on all sides by lowlands reminiscent of the Biblical wilderness that, at the Afar Depression falls sharply to below sea-level, the climate is one of stunning extremes: temperature with exhilarating mountain air in the highlands, infernal heat in parts of the fearsome lowlands.

Even the alto piano (highland) that forms part and parcel of the Great Rift Valley is not immune to immoderation. It is characterized by plunging temperatures at night and fierce downpours in kremt (winter) rainy season that makes a difference: coming and going mid-June to end of September, it determines that fat and lean years.

A Farming scene, a woman carrying insira full of water, a circular hut, thatched & walled with mud. In the background a trip to the next village.

A legend emerged from the earliest European and Arab accounts of Ethiopia as a temperate climate in the tropics, possessing a climate so pleasant that it possibly made up for the lack of contemporary health facilities. One account held that "it was only the wonderful climate of the highlands ... that checked the spread of infection and made epidemics very uncommon." Another attributed to the vehement kremt rains a municipal capability as they freshen the air and bring "cleanliness to the towns."

Together with elevation, Ethiopia's seasons dictate her agricultural activity. The seasons are not as distinctly divided as those in higher latitudes. They are bega (summer) which takes all the other seasons in its stride; belg (autumn) and midsew or spring. The capricious belg (small) rains appear for about six weeks sometime between February and April. They are harbingers of either good or bad times to come. Short and sharp, the belg rains swell river banks swell river and carry away anything in their path that is unsecured, often flooding city streets. Despite this mischief -- or because of it -- these rains hold a magic attraction for children who drench themselves, believing it will make them grow, and gamble with their personal safety in order to play in the rising torrents. They shout, "the hyena has given birth" when the sun beams through, reclaiming the sky from the clouds.

Ethiopia centers on a high, heavily dissected plateau that forces aloft monsoon winds from the Indian Ocean, cooling the air and wringing out huge quantities of rainfall. Ethiopia's rivers carry 101 billion cubic meters of water down its slopes to neighboring countries, making it truly the watershed of Africa. Dark, alluvial soil from these highlands is rushed way down the *Abai* or Blue Nile, originating at lake T'ana near the historic city of Gonder. This is joined by finer, lighter colored silts from the lake Victoria watershed, carried down the meandering White Nile. The two meet at Omduraman, near Khartoum in the Sudan. As Egypt was the "gift of the Nile", so Ethiopia was her benefactor. Within the arcking sweep of the Great Rift Valley are fresh water and salt water lakes, some clustered together and set like gems on a plush cordon of green. Abundant wildlife and waterfowl inhabit these lakes and their tributary rivers. These include diverse species of fish, pelicans, flamingos, crocodiles and hippopotamuses. Reaching out to the south, east and west are the savannah -- natural habitat of lions, panthers, elephants, buffalos, giraffes, antelopes, ostriches, zebras and wild boars.

The dissected, volcanic formation of the land -- mountains, hills, gorges, caves and flat *ambas* or mesas -- treat the eye to places among the most scenic on earth, and surprises at every turn. The late Ato Gebre Michael Kidane, whose encyclopaedic knowledge of the "soul of Ethiopia" made the country a tourist destination wrote that " the reddish and white anthills standing in the Borena plains appear like remnants of Micheangelo's marble works and are a source of curiosity and motivation for visitors."

Ethiopians classify their country into three climatic regions: *dega* (highlands) rising between 2,600 and 3,600 meters above sea level; *weiynadega*, 2,000 to 2,600 meters, and *qolla* (lowlands) from 1,400 to 2,000 meters. These divisions heavily influence demographic patterns, economic endeavors and lifestyle. Most of the population inhabits the *weiynadega*. The two climatic extremes are similar in that both are relatively barren, distinguished mainly by temperature differences and the landforms characteristic of ruthless sun in the extreme lowlands and damp, bitter cold, cloudswept crags. Both are sparsely inhabited because of the inhospitality of the land; both are given to some animal husbandry, and precious little agriculture. The physical features and clothing of the people reflect their environment. People of the *dega* wear coarse sheep wool cloaks or blankets, while inhabitants of the *qolla* wear girdled wraparounds. Both types of clothing, though different, are sturdy and well adapted to the need they must fulfill. Agriculture is the economic mainstay of the highlands, while livestock provides sustenance in the lowlands. Ethiopian peasants are hard working people who use farming techniques that have advanced little in the past many centuries. The work has become even more labor intensive as soils have been eroded and fertility depleted by farming techniques that cannot sustain the population increases Ethiopia has experienced.

Still, a variety of crops can be grown in the same geographical area because the high, intermediate and low elevations found in most parts of the country provide a variety of climatic types. A variety of crops is grown all year around, including *t'ef* (*Eragrostis abyssinica*), staple food for a good section of the population. Durra, maize (*Bahr mashella*, in Amharic), *dagusa* (finger millet), chick peas, lentils, peas, beans, oil seeds such as *nug* (*guizotia abyssinica*) and linseed, onions, garlic, coffee, tobacco, sugar, pepper and coriander are all grown as well as many types of fruits and vegetables. Interestingly, however, a traveler's observation in the last century that Ethiopians, on the whole, were "not great fruit eaters" stands to this day.

A primary dish is *we't* (a spicy stew of lamb, beef, chicken, beans or vegetables.) Like *t'ef*, *berbere* (red pepper, *Capsicum frutescens*) has always played a major part in the diet of the people. It is often the berbere that tells the story of the *we't* and gives away a bad cook. Its importance and potency is so widely recognized that a derogatory phrase *"ye wend alich'a"*

A scene in an Ethiopian kitchen, making Injera and We't.

has been coined for a man who displays cowardice. (*Ye wend alich'a* literally means a man who, like alich'a, has no pepper in him).

The *gesho* (*Rhamnus prinoides*) is another plant that brewers of *t'ella* (Ethiopian beer) and makers of *t'ej* (hydromel or mead) cannot do without.

Reputedly native to the Kefa province from which it derived its name, coffee completes the ingredients of Ethiopian hospitality. At one time coffee was consumed by Oromos and Muslims only. The clergy condemned the use of coffee. However, at a later date coffee won the palates and hearts of even the strictest of the priesthood.

Coffee did not become an intrinsic part of Ethiopian culture until the 1880s when Menelik himself drank it. At that time the Egyptian Bishop of the Ethiopian Orthodox Church, Abune Matewos, dismissed the clergy's contention that it was a Muslim drink. It is true, however, that the use of coffee was widespread in Muslim-Oromo inhabited areas from Harer through Yifat to Wello. By the early 20th century, coffee had become an export commodity. 4.2 million kilos of it was shipped to Sudan via Gambella between 1908 and 1928. It topped the list of all the export of Ethiopia and still remains number one export commodity.

Coffee drinking ceremony.

Most Ethiopians flavored their coffee with salt, butter or spices until sugar entered the scene with the Italians in 1935, According to travelers in the last century, Kefan consumers first ground the roasted beans in wooden mortars, mixed them with butter and honey, and then made them into small balls with they then placed in a pot and boiled. They frequently added spices to the concoction, to individual's taste.

Coffee-drinking in Ethiopia has a tradition all its own. While it is a ceremony of some sort, it is also a favorite pastime of the people. For centuries the art of making good coffee progressed in a leisurely fashion. Coffee beans as they come off the trees, have a bright red color and look almost like cherries. The ceremonial part of coffee making includes the art of drying the beans in the hot sun, the removal of husks from the beans. Then the beans had to be washed and dried. Then they are placed in a home-made urn or a metal pan and roasted over coals until the beans are turned to a rich, brown color, spreading their aroma to one and all in the neighborhood. They are then placed in a wooden mortar and are pounded or ground with a wooden pestle until the beans are turned into coffee powder.

Before the actual brewing of coffee takes place, fresh grass is cut and spread on the hard-baked mud floor of the house. the lady of the house squats near the door and places a pot of water on a pristine stove made generally from an oil drum and blows on the live coals with her mouth or fans it with a reed fan to keep the flames going. When the water comes to a boil, the lady adds the coffee powder and covers the pot with strands of sisal to help let off some steam and yet retain the heat.

The aroma floating through the neighborhood tantalizes the nostrils of the neighbors. Therefore, it was not unusual to have unexpected guests in one's home to participate in the ceremony of drinking coffee. When these guests join the household of the lady, oftentimes incense is burned to enhance the party mood. Not a word is spoken but everyone enjoys the aroma and awaits the serving of coffee.

The lady places some tiny coffee cups *(siniwoch)* on a four-legged wooden tray and pours a little water in each of them to be rinsed off. Rinsing was ceremonial as the cups are already washed and clean. Then the cups are filled with coffee and the tray is passed around. Coffee is served boiling hot and it is not really enjoyed unless it burns the lips of the drinkers as stated in the old adage "*ye bunna sibatu, mefajetu* " to infer "the pleasure of coffee is in its burning sensation."

Time passes slowly as each one takes a little sip of coffee while deeply engaged in village gossip or in a discussion of news. The primary or first round of sipping is called the "*abol* ." More water is added to the pot to make coffee last longer. The guests place their cups in the tray and the lady fills them up again. This is the second round called "*huletegna.*" Because of the added water to the pot, the coffee on the second round is not as thick but it is still tasty. More gossip and more story-telling goes on during the second round. In the meanwhile the lady adds more water to the pot diluting its strength. Pretty soon the cups are empty and are returned to the tray. Once again, the lady fills the cups for the third and final round. Conversation among guests hardly ceases. Although the coffee is not so thick now, it is called the "*bereka*" which means "blessing." This is the most significant of the rounds because it carries a blessing with it. Coffee-drinking sessions generally last a couple of hours and are brought to a climax by "*ye bereka bet, ye sesai bet yargew*" which means "May He make this a blessed house and a prosperous one."

Coffee picking. A typical Sidama dwelling (conical bamboo-houses) & village activities.

Ethiopia's is not a monolithic culture. Hence, "Ethiopian culture" remains a misnomer - a result of the country's political and social history over the last hundred years. Cultural integration has been attempted at various times, but its failure is thankfully due to the resilience of cultures of its constituent nationalities, each no less sophisticated than the dominant Amhara culture.

Common to all, of course, is the impact of the particular environment on the lifestyle and social organization of each cultural group. Cultural response to environmental change brought about by migration and urbanization, for example, has been one of "give-and-take" which is reflected, among other things, in costumes, hairstyles, architecture, handicrafts, and even the culinary arts.

Example of this cultural transfer -- some constructive and some destructive, are many. Just as Dorze weaving revolutionized highland fashion, so has the rigidly stratified Amhara social organization supplanted the democratic *Geda* system of the

Oromos whereby society was run by elected officers and the community at large had a say in the affairs of state.

Cultural enrichment has now brought about great mutual appreciation among Ethiopia's cultures. The need to dominate may have been reduced.

\ women Spinner & a Dorze weaver. A typical Dorze house (Bee hive shaped).

Religion is another common denominator. Christians, Muslims, Jews (Bete Israel, commonly known as Felashas) and Animists in the south have molded their social norms, behavioral patterns and world outlook according to their faiths.. Historically a partner in government, the until recently privileged Ethiopian Orthodox Church has itself left an indelible mark on the society.

Although the dietary habits and cuisine of highland Christians and Muslims differ little, if at all, both refuse to break bread together where meat is in the dish, more because of tradition than religious prohibition. At all other times, they eat out of a common platter. "*Ye Islam / Kristian siga alebelam*" (I don't eat Muslim / Christian meat!) has been standard attitude through the centuries, although both bless the animal with the monotheistic words common to both beliefs - *Be'sime Ab* (in Gi'iz) or *Bism Il-lahi* (Arabic) for "in the Name of the Father" - before they kill it.

Traveling devout Christians, Muslims, or the few Felashas who venture outside their region experience deprivation because of the prohibition. The widely traveled Englishman, C. F. Rey's account of many years ago tells the same story today.

"We had one Moslem with us when we were on the trek," he wrote, "and as he would not eat the ox which my other men had killed he bought a whole sheep for himself, and killed and ate it himself; none of the other men would touch an atom of it, even when their own supply ran out and they had no meat at all."

Such travelers also suffered much hunger in Europe because either the animal was not slaughtered according to their tradition or because of suspicion that it might be pork. Either would be considered unclean.

Such tenaciousness, though awkward in some circumstances, poignantly reflects the extent of the kosher syndrome - cleanliness of edibles - in the people's life. Meat and pulses are always washed before cooking. Equally significant, the only eating implements - the hands - have to be washed clean before touching food.

While followers of the major religions strictly observe fasts, Orthodox Christians go one farther by abstaining from all animal products for much of the year - *208 days*, including Lent and most Wednesdays and Fridays, except those immediately following Easter.

It is said a governor-general of Eritrea on a visit during Lent to the Norwegian run Naval Academy at Massawa was horrified to see cadets relishing meat dishes for which he admonished the unwitting commandant. On a second visit, the same governor found cadets enjoying everything but meat. He had to explain to the poor expatriate that abstinence also meant all animal and dairy products.

Most Orthodox Christians do not touch food or water until 3 pm on days of fasting, whereas the more lenient break fast at noon. During Passion Week, they fast until 3 pm everyday from Monday through Good Friday, and then nothing is eaten until after Mass at the break of dawn on Easter Sunday. Children under 13 are exempt, but most enjoy testing their "toughness" by doing at least half the time. Muslims and Felashas also undergo the rigors of fasting as prescribed by their faith.

A litmus test of faith occurs on Good Friday when people converge to the nearest church. Unlike other days when the faithful lean against church walls, fences, trees or tomb-stones during their communion with God, on Good Friday they perform *Sigdet* - a motion not unlike school-yard calisthenics. It entails standing erect, looking upwards to the sky, genuflecting, kissing the earth and rising again many times over with short pauses and murmurs of prayer in between. The strong, the weak and the frail partake in this collective expression of humility before the Almighty.

But *Sigdet* (bowing down before Christ after confessing sin as ordered by the priest), and its companion *nisiha* (confession), are also a "fun time" when faith and humor intermingle. The young and old the honest and the not-too-honest, confess every imaginable sin. Young men and women tease the priests with sexual innuendoes, facetiously confessing to sins like "falling from the bed last night," whereupon the priest not without humor magisterially orders, the penitent to bow a hundred times (sigdet) with repeated whisks on the shoulder with a twig.

Urbanization and, especially, Westernization of the post World War II generation introduced dramatic changes in attitude toward tradition and religion, whose effects are still felt today. Ironically, an utter disrespect for fasts launched a popular dish known as the *shifinfin* (hush hush, or wrap-up) - so-called because it was ordered in whispers and came in a deep bowl. It contain delicious meat *alich'a we't* covered with layers of *injera*, and none was the wiser for it.

Meat has always enjoyed a place of choice in the Ethiopian diet and cooking. As a selection of the choicest cheese is served after a sumptuous French dinner so is *burundo* - or in modern times, *qur't* - the choicest raw meat served at banquets or other special occasions.

C.F. Rey the English traveler wrote about one such an occasion - a royal banquet - where *burundo* was served with ceremony. Times have changed since, but the custom continues, and even the elaborate ceremony has survived, where it is seen in contemporary weddings.

He wrote:

[The guests] set to work at once on the hors-d'oeuvres, and then the *piece de resistance* arrived. Hundreds of pairs of men came in, each carrying between them a long stout pole, from which hung huge pieces of red raw meat, covered with strips of red and gold cloth.

These men stood closely together all along the tables and one on each side, so that the meat hung down from the poles over the tables just in front of the diners. The guests produced knives, and feeling the joint with their fingers to pick out a tender bit, rapidly sliced of strips of meat, which they put into their mouths, cutting off what would not go in quite close to their lips, an operation which, from personal experience, I know demands great skill if one's nose is not to suffer - as the cut is always made upwards...

The whole function had lasted nearly four hours.

Disagreements still abound about the origin of *burundo*. Some attribute it to different kings who banned lighting fire during military expeditions lest the enemy would be alerted. The troops, it is commonly believed, had no choice but to eat their meat raw which, says Rey, "may be a nourishing form of diet tending to the development of warlike qualities."

Westerners generally are prone to frown at the thought, forgetful that steak Tartar, too, is but a burundo of minced raw meat.

The appetite for meat persists, nonetheless. A European who traveled in Ethiopia during the last century asserted that "the lower class of people join together and buy a cow, which is killed and divided among them." *Qirch'a*, as the practice is called, still is common today because fresh meat is preferred over refrigerated or frozen meat. Even the well to do prefer not to buy and store a whole cow for meat. As meat traditionally was not sold in shops, any extra meat purchased was preserved by drying. The result was *qwan'ta*, and ideal *we't* ingredient, a wayfarer's provision, or simply a snack for visitors.

After lamb, poultry is preferred over other meats. Relatively affordable at markets, chickens are also raised in yards, demanding iittle yet always available for a festive occasion. Together with tomatoes, pepper and other vegetables growing in the compound, the scene is set for a varied menu.

Great skill is required to prepare a chicken into *doro we't*. Twelve parts must be artfully cut and a dozen hard boiled eggs immersed to absorb the spiced gravy that tells the world a special is on the stove. After the Italian occupation, *doro we't* was referred to as the plane with its bombs.

The smell of *doro we't* signifies that a guest is expected. The cook takes great pains to make it savory - *ij yemiyasme'ti't* (a dish that makes you lick your fingers). This only tells you how good it is, as to lick your fingers is a social gaffe.

Historically and to this day, the skill of the potter is a decisive factor in Ethiopian cooking. As earthenware pots yield the best taste, no we't worth its salt is cooked in anything else. The makers, invariably women, hardly ever employ potters' wheels, yet they produce perfectly round pots or other handsome utensils which they fire for impermeability. Despite their skill, however, potters have been relegated to a low station in Ethiopian society.

Basketware, on the other hand, was a special skill any wife would be proud of. The *mesob* - a basket-table - for serving food was often her own handiwork. To waterproof it she would use *qulqwal* - aloe - juice, which, incidentally, is also widely used for medical purposes. To make an *agelgil* - a kind of picnic basket - she would bind it with tanned leather and adds a strap around it to facilitate ease of carrying. Other such domestic products are parasols, straw hats, and other goods.

> Many years ago, a foreign traveler wrote:
> The females work very well in grass; some of the baskets are beautifully made of different grass and fibres-let in in patterns. The dish covers are also handsome and show great taste; they are also woven of grass ornamented with kid skin, dyed red, green, blue and yellow. The grass bottles and bowls are perfectly water-tight, and I have seen the latter placed near the embers of the fire to keep the food contained therein warm without doing the article any harm.

Basket weaving (Mesob) by a Hareri woman. Market activities in the old wall city of Harer.

The architecture of an Ethiopian house will vary with the regions. Some are simple, round mud huts with thatched roofs and invariably one-room abodes with mud floors. How Europeans came to call them "Tukuls" remains a mystery.

In the south, among the Sidama the conical bamboo-houses present a delightful picture of extraordinary aesthetics. The space between rows of houses surrounded by enset (false banana) trees is no less a boulevard with its sheer width and geometric layout than any in a Western capital.

Up north in Tigrai, the dwellings - *hidmo* - are skillfully constructed with stone, often up to two storeys high, and are naturally air-conditioned. The Adere homes in Harer are concentrated within a walled city not unlike the Casbah of Algiers or Marrakesh.

The interior of the house is often laid out to serve many different purpose, according to the time of day - a sitting room, kitchen and bedroom, the *medeb* - a built-in stone structure the height of a settee with layers of animal skin cover playing the role of a sofa-bed. In brief, the abodes are no less compact than Western studio apartments.

Though she may be not equal to her man in Western feminist terms, the homemaker is the "crown of her husband."

Neither displays outward signs of affection, but both employ a gesture here, a tender tone of voice there, and other forms of subtle communication which confirm their love for each other. When he flirts and she says no, she means yes. It is only a game of love.

Mutual respect is central in marriage. A man who lacks it becomes an object of derision in his community.

Customary law entitles the wife to retain her prenuptial assets upon marriage - a prerogative that guarantees her equality in the home. And more significantly, she retains her maiden name. She can divorce her husband as easily as he can terminate the marriage which, Rey rightly observed, "gives her a certain protection in itself."

"In spite of the facility of divorce - possibly to some extent because of the mutual power to exercise it," went on the Englishman, "the lot of the women is not at all what one might expect; they are by no means ... hewers of wood and drawers of water."

In a traditional setting, the wife never mentions her husband by name: if she had to, she would call the name of one of her sons. When the son responds, she says: "I don't mean you, I

A typical tigral dwelling, hidmo. Far right women crushing grains.

mean your father." When she speaks to him she would use the second person plural - *irswo* (the equivalent of the French *vous* or the German *Sie*). In his absence, it would always be in the third person polite *isachew*, (roughly, they.) For example, she might say *isachew qebir hedewal*: they went to the funeral. Privately or out of earshot, however, she would simply address him as *ante*, as in the French *tu* or the German *Du*. It would be such lady who would welcome you as a guest to her home. The food is already cooked. She has swept the mud floor clean. Nothing is left to chance. Maybe it is *Inqut'at'ash* - New Year. The family would be wearing new clothes. If not *yekit libs* (Sunday clothes) would do. They have been stored away in a bag of kid skin - *Silicha* - hanging on the wall.

Earlier in the week, the couple would have done the family's laundry in a stream with *inddod* (pircunia abyssinica) - an unimpressive plant with detergent properties that grows on river bands and was made famous by Ethiopian scientist Aklilu Lemma as an effective medicine against Bilharziasis. And the night before - the 5th or 6th of Pagume - the family would have bathed in the cold water of the stream.

Until the import-export trade made cotton inaccessible and weavers redundant, even the lowliest of families could afford a new outfit on New Year. As the saying goes, *le Inqut'at'ash yalhone qemis, yibet'at'es.* (literally, let the skirt waste if I wont get it for New Year.) It now expresses frustration at delayed help or expectation.

Imagine you are visiting from a 'distant village', say a hundred miles away. Having just arrived, you have had to cross a river swollen by torrential rains as the *kremt* rainy season is well underway. In your crossing, you had to use a *gerbeta* or *jandis* - large inflated bags of ox skin - or possibly you crossed it on a raft "made of pieces of drift-wood lashed together and rendered buoyant by inflated hides and water skins". Then you had to travel the rest of the way on foot or mule back. As you arrived, you were expected. The master of the house in his new white *kuta* is sitting outside on a - *berch'uma* - a stool carved out of a tree trunk, maybe inside.

No matter. You holler: *Betoch* ! (Those in the house.) And the wife answers back: *Dejoch* ! (Those outside [come in]).

Effusive greetings follow. You are saying "*bet l'embosa* ", (May freshness come to the house!) as you enter. Etiquette demands haggling about the seat" you insist on the stool, and they on the *medeb* , or sofa. You give up and sit where you are shown.

You notice the beautiful dress your hostess is wearing. You want to make compliments, so you steer the conversation to articles of clothing, maybe the price of *abujedid* - calico. When you say the *kuta* is handsome it is understood the compliment is for her. It is unbecoming to compliment a woman in general, most of all, another man's wife.

The wife: "*ye'bet fetil new.*" (It is home spun.) The proud husband picks up the thread to add: "*Iswa wanna balemoy nat.*" (She is a skillful spinner.)

Indeed she would be, like all her other sisters throughout the country. She had bought the unprocessed cotton at the weekly market where she went to sell her own farm produce. She had picked out the seeds and flattened the cotton on flintstone with a metal bar, and then twined the white material by tweaking the string of a bow. The knots thus formed were spun with a horn or, as the case may be, an ivory-tipped *inzirt* (spindle) made of reed.

To achieve that she had to "hold the fleecy cotton in her left hand and lift it to its furthest extent while with her right she would operate the reed which she would rotate on her bare thigh, the thickness of the thread depending on the speed at which the cotton was drawn out."

She had then transferred the thread onto spools made of reed that she used to make the outfit the couple are wearing. Hers is a matching combination of white *net'ela* a thinner version of her husband's - and *qemis* (skirt) each with a beautiful border patterned with a variety of colors.

The *weiyzero* (Mrs. or lady) has also other attributes to display: her *shurubba* (plaited hair), done the day before, is stunning: lines of hair knotted cornrow fashion with the end resting elegantly over her neck "done in a chignon" to form, in Rey's words, "a becoming frame to the face."

Plaiting is a painful operation since the hair has to be pulled hard and held tight throughout the process. *Il faut souffrir pour être beau*, was the remark of the appreciative traveler.

Costumes & hair styles.

No doubt the *weiyzero* had the night before rested her head on a *birkuma* - a handsomely decorated wooden "pillow" curved to take the neck to avoid dishiveling her beautiful coiffure. A head rest not unlike the Ethiopian *burkuma* was discovered in Tutankhamen's tomb in Egypt, which shows that the humble object is rooted in antiquity.

You notice, too that she has buttered her head which goes with spirit of the holidays, but the practice is equally common as an excellent ointment for thinning hair.

Rey quotes a Mansfield Parkyns who lived in Ethiopia who, he said, "used no head covering of any sort at any time other than a coating of butter, which he says he found as effective as any hat."

Touched and lined with *kul* (mascara), her eyelashes and brows have enhanced her beauty. Like all other Ethiopian, except the few "moderns", she is not wearing any other makeup, but she smells of myrrh. She had immersed her feet and hands into a not so lukewarm bowl of *insosila* (henna, *impatiens tinctoria*) the night before, which has tanned her finger- and toenails and browned her palms. Finally, she has rubbed her teeth white with charcoal and tattooed her gums.

All the guests have now gathered and lunch must now be served, but first the hands must be washed. Her son comes forward and the visitors hold him by the chin and kiss him thrice on the cheeks as if to raise him after he had stooped with the utmost display of respect to kiss them on the knee. He has a tuft of hair - *qunch'o* - near the forehead of his shaven scalp. Girls his age would have hair all round their head with the center completely shaven called *gamé*. The bare area will be left to grow hair as the girls reach marriageable age. Other boys would have *telela* - a juvenile hair style - that Rey said "gives the appearance of a cock's comb and is most comical." He would not have been amused had he seen modern day punks sporting a *telela* - "the head bare except for a strip of hair extending from the back of the neck to the forehead over the center of the head."

The boy was circumcised when he was only seven-days-old following a ritual practised, says Gibbons, "by the most ancient Ethiopians, from motives of health and cleanliness." A girl would undergo clitoridectomy between the ages of eight and twelve. In some parts of the country, infibulation would also be performed on her.

As the lady of the house rises you would soon notice her long *qemis* (homespun dress) reach her ankles, each adorned by *albo*, or anklets of tiny round silver balls strung together. At other times she wears anklets made of beads of different colors. Around her wrist are *ambars*, bracelets that perfectly match her anklets.To complete her jewelry, she is wearing silver earrings.

She places the *mesob* by the *medeb*, towards which those seated on the stools huddle. Before lunch *t'ella* a home made beer, would have been served in a *wanch'a*, a tumbler made of horn (mostly buffalo) or clay. Otherwise it may be served in an imported enamelled iron mug, imprinted with Emperor Menelik's picture. Or *t'ej*, a honey mead, may be served in *birile*.

The couple's son would be squatting in a corner to eat his lunch as the adults wine and dine. Had it been supper, he would be standing by the *mesob* holding a crudely made lamp as long as the meals lasted.

In his excellent <u>Travels in Ethiopia</u>, the Briton, David Buxton conveys best a European's first experience at an Ethiopian dinner table. His host, the district governor, first "plied me with *te'j*, the local honey-wine," he says and asked him to stay for lunch:

> At the time I had little experience of Ethiopian fare, but soon acquired the taste for it and afterwards welcomed every opportunity to share a local meal. In time I could tell my Ethiopians friends that I preferred their own drinks to any European liquor -which was true, though I think they seldom believed it.
>
> For a while we sat drinking *t'ej* from *biriles*, small decanter-shaped bottles with narrow necks which are usually preferred to tumblers in Ethiopia ...
>
> The women of the household were busily preparing our meal. Piles of *injera* - the local bread which takes the form of thin round sheets like pancakes - were stacked ready. *Wat*, the highly-peppered sauce that accompanies it, was boiling in earthenware bowls and a most savoury smell began to pervade the room.
>
> As this was a modernized household, plates were laid, and to the right of each plate an *injera* was neatly folded up, like a napkin. Before we started a servant brought round a jug of water for the hand-washing ritual; the water was dribbled over each person's hands in turn. Our host's wife then doled out *wat* on to the plates. There is only one way of eating *watt* and *injera*. You tear a small piece from your sheet of *injera* (etiquette requires that the right hand only should be used), mop up a little *wat* with this and put it in your mouth. It is particularly a tasty combination, and the *habitué* has only to think of it for his mouth to water. But I found it, as every European does at first, so burning-hot with red pepper that I sweated profusely and tried to cool it off with *t'ej*, which only made it burn my mouth

more fiercely. Other sorts of *wat* were brought, with bits of chicken and hard-boiled eggs. The meal over, water was again brought round for hand washing, which was now very necessary. Later black coffee was brewed.

It was one such home that a European is said to have put the *injera* in his lap thinking it was a napkin.

Rey and his wife discovered the *injera* to be "very good, especially when eaten with jam and butter."

In a traditional household the meal would be served on a common platter or, as described above, a *mesob*. However the meal is served, the mistress of the house would tear a sizeable piece from the "sheet of *injera*" artfully roll it up full of meat and sauce, and offer to feed you a *gursha*, which appears at first to be a small morsel held in the finger tips.

She would do it the second time ignoring you nays. Despite your repeated *beqans* (I am full), she would insist "*hulet yat'alal.*" (Twice causes disharmony.) It is not clear why it has to be three times, but it could be a reference to the Trinity; which would be in total disharmony solo or duo.

In Muslim households no alcoholic beverages are served, but spiced tea, coffee and *birz* (a gentle, delicious drink made of honey and water) complete a sumptuous meal. These drinks are often followed with deserts, including *halawa* (baklava) or fruits.

By tradition hospitality is obligatory. It simply is a second nature to the Ethiopian. Perhaps because of it, inns and eating places were non-existent. The nearest to a hospitality business were the urban *mesheta-bets* (drinking houses) in commercial centers which locals and travelers frequented. Their female owners were not especially of excellent repute!

When a *ye'gzer mengedegna* (God's wayfarer) chanced into a village he was fed and lodged. Where there where no children or servants the mistress of the house washed his feet. If he had pack animals, his hosts unloaded them and provided feed for his beasts.

One European traveler wrote of his first experience with Ethiopian hospitality in a village. He had arrived with a caravan and decided to rest his weary feet until the inhabitants away in their fields, returned at sundown. To his horror, so it seemed to him they simply passed him by.

A scene from a Gurage village: Form of farming, circular houses with thatched steep roofs with a pot at the apex. Surrounded by False Banana. Women scraping Qoch'o.

I thought," he says, "their going straight in saying nothing rather impolite: but sill this was excusable, as no doubt they were much fatigued, and must have their supper before they could attend to us. However, I was not long left in suspense. Immediately on their entry there was a great bustle and moving of skins and other articles of furniture. Meanwhile one of the boys who had gone in with the others came out again, bringing me a large bowl of new milk to drink... [A respectable-looking man] politely ushered me into the house. The bustle we had heard was occasioned by their placing skins, a couch, etc. in the best hut, and removing some corn-jars and other utensils which had formerly occupied it. Having himself arranged the couch for me, he seated

me on it; and then going out brought us a good
supply of provisions, serving me with his own
hands, and putting into my mouth the very supper which no doubt was intended for himself.

Again by tradition Ethiopians are socially active. They
turn others' weddings into collective joy. They help cook, serve,
and sing and dance. They share the pains and sorrows of others.
They help with burial costs, attend funerals, and comfort the be-
reaved with daily visits for a week.

If Christians, they form a *mahber*, "society for private
communion", Buxton calls them, to commemorate a favorite
saint, from which there are too many too choose to many to
name. Although meetings are opened with prayers by priests,
mahbers are, for all intents and purposes, parties with plenty to
eat and drink, highlighted by the *dabbo*, the thick wheat bread
that is eighteen inches in diameter. Its baking, if good, enhances
a woman's reputation as mistress of the culinary arts.

The get-together is held in the houses of members in ro-
tation, on the same monthly saint's day. The *mahber* has also
other social functions: it operates, among other things, as a mutual aid society to help members having difficulties, including
marital problems.

Each day of the month is assigned a saint. "If all these
were recognized as holidays," wrote Buxton, "scarcely any work
would ever be done."

Ethiopia's is what is best known as Julian Calendar, created by Julius Caesar in 46 B.C., which, still unbeknown to most
Westerners, was also in use in Europe until the late 1700s. The
year is divided into twelve months of thirty days each. The remaining five (six in a leap year) days make a mini-month ('Pagume) , hence the realistic tourist slogan, "Ethiopia, 13 months
of sunshine".

The first of Meskerem, which normally corresponds to
the Gregorian (European) 11th of September, marks *Inqut'at'ash*
(New Year). The odd ' Pagume's fifth or sixth day thus becomes
New Year's Eve. The twelve months coincide with the lunar year
and the thirteenth month, 'Pagume, is added to make the calendar year to conform with the solar year.

From 1st Meskerem (11 September) to 31 December in the Gregorian Calendar, the Ethiopian Calendar is seven years behind. From 1 January (Gregorian) to 5 or 6 'Pagume (Julian), the gap becomes eight years. So, for the foreigner in Ethiopia it is like growing younger, and for the Ethiopian like growing older.

The calendar has four-year cycle each named after one of the four Evangelists: Matthew, Mark, Luke and John. The reason behind the cycle of Evangelists is a mystery. So is the origin of *Inqut'at'ash* itself.

Some believe there is kinship between the Ethiopian calendar and that of ancient Egypt which is said to have originated as early as the fourth millennium.

Rey was right when he said "in endeavoring to translate dates from Abyssinian to European computation bad snags await the unwary."

In the first place," he says, "the introduction of the 6th 'Pagume in their leap year throws all the dates between September and the following February back a day. The Abyssinian year following their leap year (which incidentally precedes ours!) begins on the 12th September instead of 11th September and continues a day behind time until our 29th February, when it is automatically readjusted. And if the translator wishes to compare dates prior to the present century he will find further joys in store for him.

For the Abyssinians," he goes on, "have counted as leap years the three years we do not (though they are properly leap years), viz.: 1700, 1800 and 1900. Nor do they take account of the additional day we dropped in 1800, nor, I think, of the ten days omitted from our calendar in 1582. So they gradually picked up fourteen days out of seven (or eight) years that They were (and are) behind. This probably explains why their year starts on 11th September instead of 29th August, as in the case of most Eastern nations.

Rey further observes that the difference in the number of years between the Ethiopian computation and that of the European is possibly due, firstly, to the Ethiopians' adoption of the Alexandrian Era recognizing 5500 years from the creation to the birth of Christ, which was placed three years before that given by the Dionysian Era (i.e., 5502 B.C. 29th August); and, secondly, the Diocletian era which dropped ten years out of the calendar in A.D. 284, thus losing ten years and gaining three or two according to the dates to be computed.

A similar result would have been attained had the Ethiopians adopted, in stead the calculation made by the Egyptian monk Ponodorus who (circa A.D. 400) struck ten years off the age of the world and placed the Incarnation three years after the then accepted date thus forming the 'Mundane Era of Antioch' which was adopted by the Christians of Syria."

Be that as it may, in September the entire country is in a festive spirit for the new year celebration, as it is the end of *kremt* when, says the observant Buxton,

the sun is peculiarly welcome after its partial retirement during the rains, and the flowers, only waiting, as it were, for the excessive rain to stop, lie ready to come out with a rush, In the first few weeks of the year the highland pastures turn to gold as the maskal daisies come out - pretty flowers whether singly or in the mass, each yellow petal flecked with orange.

After dark on New Year's Eve people gather at their doors and light little fires, and children may run about carrying burning torches. On New Year's day itself parties of girls come round singing special songs, hoping for a tip and children offer branches of grass and flowers. The grass is known as *inkwutatash*, so is the whole bouquet or other present given at this time, so is the New Year itself. This is the time for exchanging formal New Year greetings, whether by word of mouth or by letter.

For travelers time is an equally confusing aspect of Ethiopian life. The day is divided into twelve hours of sunlight and twelve hours darkness. The morning starts at 1 o'clock, (7 am European time). Noon is 6 o'clock and the day ends at sunset - 12 o'clock, or 6 pm. Night comes at 1 o'clock (7pm) and lasts until 12 o'clock (6 am).

New Year eve Demera

There are many holidays that have affinity to the rest of the Christian world: for example, Christmas (the 7th or 8th of January), and Easter (variable). However, some Christian holidays have, because of the country's political history since the last century, become mainstream festivals.

Mesqel, which commemorates the finding of the True Cross by St. Helena comes in the wake of the New Year in September. On its eve, a *demera* - a tall pole - is set up at a public square to which many more are added with their ends decorated with *Mesqel* daisies, thus forming an impressive pyramid. The crowds, including local dignitaries led by priests in ceremonial attire, encircle it three times as evening approaches when it is set alight to make a "splendid bonfire."

Genna (Christmas) is a subdued affair enlivened only by a game of the same name. *Genna* resembles hockey and is played with bent sticks (*t'ing*). The ball *(irur)* is a rounded chunk of wood which can be fatal if it strikes a player or spectator. There are no rules, nor is there a limit to the number of players or a properly delimited pitch. The goals could be any two spots, even two villages. And competing villages play the game almost non-stop for up to three days.

Gugs (equestrian game) being played by horse men. Two children playing Genna.

Also customary during the Ethiopian Christmas celebration is the *genna dabbo*, a special Christmas bread, which is baked with the love, respect and skill the occasion commands.

The festival of "riotous rejoicing", however, is the carnival-type *Timqet* (Epiphany) which commemorates the Baptism of Christ. On its eve, the *tabots* (Arks of Covenant) of each church "spend the night outside" in an open field not far from a pool from where the priests sprinkle the crowd with holy water.

Describing the three days of *Timqet* (18th, 19th, and 20th January), Rey has this to say about this "perhaps the most beautiful and remarkable of their various pageants":

It is difficult in mere words to do justice to the really wonderful pageantry attendant on these religious festivals. Their historical significance alone is worth of the pen of Gibbon, for they are probably some 3000 years old in some of their features, and half-closing one's eyes it is possible to imagine the picture before one to be that of David, his priests, and his courtiers dancing before the ark, as the priests in their centuries-old vestments sway and swing before the modern representation of the Ark of the Covenant.

On the day itself, it is dance and music everywhere, some women going into a trance because they become possessed by the *zar* - the spirit.

As the church processions head home, *gugs* (equestrian game) is played in which horsemen display their skills in horse riding (some bareback) and in throwing wands like spears against each other at a fantastic speed. [Excellent horsemen hold to the mane of their mount to run side by side with their galloping horse, and then remount with breath-taking skill.] Extremely exciting, yes, but horsemen are known to have died of injuries from falls or from the flying wands.

August 19 each year right in the middle of the rainy season, children have their own festival, *Buhe*, a name derived from the Gi'iz, the ancient language, which means "He revealed himself."

As legend has it, Christ and his disciples climbed Mt. Tabor (Eromonium) on that date with his disciples to pray. Young shepherds who saw light went up the mountain to check. When the children failed to return late at night, their worried families formed a search party with lighted torches and took along *dabbo* (bread) for them. In commemoration of this story, *dabbo* and torches are part of the children's festival.

On *Buhe* day, children group together carrying lighted torches and sing outside people's homes, and the occupants gave them pieces of bread, money and other gifts.

Incidentally, *dabbo* is also served at weddings as a symbol of the bride's virginity. It is sliced from the center out to again

I

symbolize that soon she will be a woman. As part of the tradition, in-laws pay homage to each other exchanging *dabbo* as gifts.

Many facets of Ethiopian life in modern times portrayed on parchments and canvas by artists who often have religious background. What is known as "Ethiopian art" is religious art that, with time, has developed into folk art. It was the scribes (*debteras*) of the Orthodox Church who specialized in and refined the characteristic Ethiopian style as they illustrated holy books. Then secular artists adopted and further developed the style. Departure from religious subjects usually took the form of depict monarchs in martial postures, and hardly any activities during times of peace.

Out of the religious art developed a comic-strip type of pictorial narration, often centered on the Queen of Sheba legend, complete with brief captions. When this particular art form developed is still unclear. However, some artists moved to painting village scenes that simply, colorfully and impressively tell about daily lives of their communities. More often, however, they depict war, hunting and other macho activities which, in many ways, reflect the male dominance of traditional societies.

The technique is as simple as the story which is always captioned. The preparation of materials including paint and parchment, is the hard part but also most sophisticated. The paint is made of plant pigments and the vellum often is kidskin.

****

Much of the life style and tradition described above has changed dramatically since the overthrow of Emperor Haile Selassie events of 1974. However, the soul of the nation is still unscathed and traditions that may now be latent will certainly reemerge as they are permitted to. Ethiopia is a peasant country, and its heart is in the land. Politics may have affected the visible lifestyle but not the tradition that is held in the heart, a product of many centuries.

T'ef

the Lovegrass the Ethiopians have never done without

Teff, a cereal grain until now unique to Ehiopia, is more than an edible seed for the Ethiopians. It is the main food component of their cultural identity.

Ethiopian botanist Melak H. Mengesha asserts that "the earliest use of teff seeds for human consumption is lost in antiquity." That only Ethiopians—an ancient people with uninterrupted history—love the "Lovegrass" as their staple may reveal quite a bit about the origins of the culture and its agriculture. Like the country's people, Teff is diverse in habitat and color, not homogineized for production like modern grains. The wild ancestors of Teff lived here in the area of earliest human evolution. The seeds of these grasses were undoubtedly gathered by these early humans.

Until recently the production of Teff exceeded all other cereal crops combined. Sadly, recent history and government policy have put emphasis on collective production of cash crops. This is having dire effects on the nutritionaly and culturally viable grain. "Ad organizations", says American whole foods specialist Rebecca T Wood "provide high-yield chemical requiring seed of other crops that have economic value in the world market . . . These destructive practices have caused the loss of many valuable Teff varieties—as well as of the culture itself.

Teff, Eragrostis tef., is a member of a grass genus known as Eragrostis or lovegrass (from the Greek eros or love and agrostis or grass.) It has many wild relatives around the world, including the American plains where Sand Lovegrass thrives, once a favorite of the Buffalo.

Cultivation of Teff in the U.S. has been pioneered by Wayne Carlson of Maskal Forages in Idaho. "We specialize in bringing valuable, nutritious foods that the tides of history have passed by, to market." Says Carlson "We think of them as vital egg baskets, each contributing a strand to the life support system."

Teff is versatile and adaptable, yet quite demanding to grow. It is labor intensive. The sheer weight of the seeds bend the stems to the ground where they fall pell mell. It is a classic example of no pain, no gain. The gain in this case is superior nutritional value and undeniably excellent flavor—a delight to the health food enthusiast.

Wood rightly calls Teff the "super grain" because it is a "nutritional powerhouse." It's iron content is two to three times that of wheat, barley or grain sorghum. Research shows that it has 14% protein 3% fat and 81% complex carbohydrate. The calcium, potassium and other essential minerals are also many times the concentration of other grains.

Teff also is the only grain to have a symbiotic yeast according to Fred C. Meyers of the National Arboritum in Washington D.C. The yeast is right on the grain, much like that of grapes, and stays right with it into the kitchen.

Teff is milled to flour and made into a batter like dough. This is baked into injera the staple of the highlands. Injera always has a slight sour dough taste that complements the spices used in Ethiopian cuisine, and no meal worth its salt is without it. This may explain why Ethiopians do not go for desserts. Injera plays the double role of companion to tasty wet and the cheese served to crown a French dinner.

Teff is now available through the health and gourmet food distribution chain or directly from Maskal Forages Inc. 1318 Willow Street, Caldwell Idaho 83605 (208) 454-3330

Red Peppers

Important ingredients in many Ethiopian dishes are the vegetables known as peppers. The pepper family has many varieties, ranging from the sweet-tasting red or green bell pepper to the mouth burning serrano.

Other members of the family include:

The purple and golden (Holland) versions of the bell pepper;

The Cubanelle, sometimes called the "Italian frying pepper," is a sweet thick-fleshed pepper that is most often eaten split and fried in oil until tender, always with garlic;

Ancho peppers, also known as "poblano", are dark green, mildly hot, and the variety used for making the favorite Mexican dish, Chilies Rellanos;

The cayenne peppers, grown and used worldwide, vary in size from 2 to 12 inches, may be served fresh or dried, ripe (red) or immature (green), and all are hot;

Santa Fe Grande peppers, also known as yellow wax and sweet pickle, may be either sweet or hot, come in a variety of colors, and are often prepared commercially as pickled peppers.

The three varieties of peppers most frequently used in Ethiopian cookery are: (1) the Anaheim, (2) the Jalapeño, and (3) the Serrano.

The Anaheim, also known as the California green chile, adds a mild touch of heat to food. Jalapeño peppers are probably the most popular and the best known hot pepper of the family. For those who have developed a tolerance for eating hot peppers, the jalapeño is considered rather mild; the novice who wants to add a little zip to his meals chops or slices the pickled version into a range of dishes.

Considered one of the hottest peppers by Northern Americans, the Serrano pepper is very popular in Ethiopian dishes.

Most of the peppers described above can be found in most American supermarkets, or if not, then in Latin American or other ethnic grocery stores. When shopping for peppers, look for plump, firm ones that are blemish-free and have a bright color- ful, fresh appearance.

Precaution should be taken in handling and preparing pep- pers to avoid irritation and burning of skin, eyes, and mouth. The seeds and veins of the peppers contain the chemical "capsicin," which causes the irritation. Some cooks suggest wearing thin plastic gloves to prepare peppers, but others say that using a paring knife to carefully cut and scrape seeds and veins can also avoid problems. Rubbing alcohol is thought to be more effective than soap and water in removing the stinging oils from hands.

Store peppers loosely in the refrigerator so that cool moist air can circulate and keep them fresh and plump for at least a week.

King Onion

Onions have a regal place in all Ethiopian cooking. Most ideal is the oval, deep purplish and mild Italian bulb which is also excel- lent for salads.

In all your cooking, except when you cook *alich'a* (mild) dishes, make sure that you brown onions without adding oil or butter. This needs your undivided attention to avoid scorching your most vital cooking ingredient. Add a few drops of water as they start to dry to maintain gradual brownness. The procedure to follow after that is given in each recipe.

What To Know About Cooking Oil

OIL, but not too much of it, is an essential ingredient of Ethiopian cooking. Homemade rapeseed and sunflower oil was widely used before modern times when industrial oil became an economical alternative, but countryfolk are still oiling their cooking in the best of cottage industry traditions.

Health-conscious Westerners are now concerned about **cholesterol contents** of all food products and would have their minds at rest if they knew that no vegetable oil contains the dreaded cholesterol. For that, the risk is to be sought and found in animal products. Ethiopian fasting dishes, which are essentially vegetarian, use oil but in small quantity.

Dieticians point out that all vegetable oils contain "*saturated, polyunsaturated fatty acid.*" However, consumers will have to be aware of hydrogenation, although partial, of some oils to extend shelf life, the effects of which have yet to be determined.

On the other hand, oils, mostly coconut, palm kernel and palm, contain saturated fat with dire consequences such as coronary heart diseases. This is so because the fats contribute to retention of cholesterol in our body derived from consumption of animal products. The complications include atheroscelotsis, an artery-clogging condition.

Oils with minimal, i.e., less than one-third saturated fat, are called *unsaturates.* These are also commonly called *polyunsaturated fats* that are believed to lower cholesterol levels in the blood.

The oils that Ethiopian cuisine uses—cottonseed, safflower, sunflower, corn, soyabean and the like—contain linoeic acid that the body needs to make its own fat.

Monounsaturated fats lower artery damage and are widely believed not to cause cancer.

The temperature to which oil can be heated in the process of cooking is called smoke point. Oil tends to discolor at smoke point, but it poses no adverse effect on health. Central, however, is the cooking time that if long oxidizes the oil and produce lipids that irritate the arteries and creates sites for atherosclerotic deposits. Reason why reuse of cooking oil is not advisable.

Experts counsel storing cooking oil in refrigerated condition to avoid and retard oxidization that produces rancidity. Manufacturers claim that refrigerated oils should last a year.

In terms of dietary consideration, oils contain vitamin E, a natural antitoxicant.

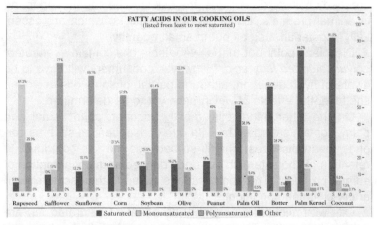

Reprinted by permission from Food & Wine Magazine, *February 1989. Copyright © 1989 by Amex Food & Wine Magazine Corporation.*

Sharing the Secrets of Professional Cooks

Tips for Easy Cooking

ETHIOPIAN cooking is delicate and time consuming. The smart cook must, therefore, make the selection of her recipe basing on the time available to prepare that special dish; the sophistication, status or number of her guests; and, of course, the ingredients she would be using and the time she would be envisaging for the dinner to last.

In Ethiopian cooking time is of the essence. A good cook will determine beforehand whether the food will be stewed, stir-fried, fried, grilled, or steamed. That will tell her how much time she has on her hands. Her second, but important, step is to prepare the ingredients according to the recipe and assemble the required utensils. For efficiency make sure to clean up as you cook.

Knowledge of the different methods of cooking will also make your task less arduous and more enjoyable. For the secret of good cooking lies in mastering its basic principles.

Stewing—cooking food over low heat in small amounts of warm water in a covered cooking pot.

Stir frying—cooking equal size cut meat, etc. in small amount of fat over high heat, first adding ingredient with the longest cooking time. Stir constantly.

Frying—cooking in hot fat for food to sizzle gently. Avoid crowding the pan to let food absorb the fat.

Grilling—cooking meat placed on the rack from the bottom heat.

Steaming—cooking over boiling liquid in a tightly covered pot.

Roasting—cooking meat and poultry uncovered in a closed oven. Pre-heat oven for 15 to 25 minutes.

Doing It Right

Meats

*Match cut of meat to type of cooking. For quick cooking use dry heat method for tender cuts. Simmer tougher meat for good results.
*Keep meat at room temperature before cooking.
*For better browning, pat surface of meat to dry.
*Start cooking at high temperature to produce a crusty browned exterior.
*Let meat stand loosely covered with foil for 10–15 minutes to retain juice before carving.
*Use tongs to turn meat. Piercing with a fork will drain the juices.

Poultry

*Rinse bird in running cold water and rub with lemon.
*Dry thoroughly and keep bird at room temperature before cooking.

Fish

*Rinse fish in running cold water and rub with lemon.
*Do not overcook.

Vegetables

*Rinse thoroughly before cooking or preparing.
*Do not overcook or undercook vegetables.
*Give lift by squeezing lemon juice over cooked vegetables.

Storing Prepared
and
Unprepared Foods

Injera and **bread** is best stored in a basket or a plastic container. Both can be refrigerated for longer period of time.

Cereals and **legumes** are best stored in a cool dry place in tightly closed jar.

Berbere, shiro, herbs and **spices:** In order to prevent oxidation which decreases the flavor, color and aroma, they are best stored in a tight opaque container such as amber glass and placed away from direct light.

Since temperature fluctuations can cause condensation, excessive moisture will wear off the flavor. Therefore, storing them at below 70 degrees is highly recommended.

Shelf life for each herb varies because much of the flavor comes from the plants' volatile oils that evaporate or oxidize. Other factor that determines storage condition is the form of the spices. Spices that have been cut or powdered will lose their flavor more rapidly than those that are in their natural form.

For long term storage, including freezing, use glass jars with a tight lid.

Vegetables

Consumption of vegetables must be immediate. If stored, they should be kept in cool places and refrigerated or covered with plastic sheets.

Meats, poultry and fish

Fresh meat, poultry and fish should be kept in the refrigerator uncovered or loosely covered. If cooked, they should be kept covered.

Milk and Byproducts

Milk and byproducts should be stored in a clean covered container and refrigerated.

How To Prepare Basic Ingredients

In preparing basic ingredients, it is economical and convenient to buy the spices in larger amounts, prepare them and store them in labeled, tightly closed containers. So as not to lose its flavor and aroma, preparing enough spices to last three month is the safest thing to do.

Ethiopian cooking requires a variety of spices. And skillfully and carefully prepared and mixed spices make *we't* what it should be.

Berbere must be stored in opaque, rust-proof containers in a cupboard away from direct light to preserve its color and substance. In a refrigerator, also away from the light, also preserves its freshness and lifespan. If available, clay pots make excellent storage containers.

HOW TO PREPARE BARLEY FLOUR

YEGEBS DUQET

UTENSILS: medium mixing bowl
mortar and pestle
medium roasting pan

INGREDIENTS:

4 cups	barley seeds
1 Tbsp.	fenugreek powder
1/2 cup	garlic powder
1/2 cup	ginger powder
to taste	salt
6 cups	water

PREPARATION: Soak overnight 4 cups *barley seeds* in 6 cups of *water*. Drain and discard water and rub barley by hand. Spread out to dry. Roast dried barley lightly in medium roasting pan on low heat for 15 minutes. Cool and pound barley gently and remove the skin. Grind to fine powder and mix the *spices* well with the barley seeds. Store powder in a tight container in dry place and use as needed.

Yegebs Duqet is used in the preparation of Yegebs Siljo, or Yegebs Injera and Yegebs Qitta, a vital ingredient used in brewing T'ella.

Barley

HOW TO PREPARE BROAD BEANS FLOUR

YEBAQELA DUQET

UTENSILS: medium mixing bowl
mortar and pestle (for pounding)
medium frying pan

INGREDIENTS: 4 cups   broad beans
1/2 cup   garlic powder
1/2 cup   ginger powder
to taste   salt
6 cups   water

PREPARATION: Soak overnight 4 cups *broad beans* in 6 cups of *water*. Drain and discard water and rub broad beans by hand. Spread out to dry. Roast dried broad beans lightly in medium frying pan on low heat for 15 minutes. Cool and pound broad beans gently and remove pods. Grind to a fine powder and mix the *spices* well to the broad beans. Store powder in a tight container in dry place and use as needed.

Yebaqela Duqet is used in the preparation of Yebaqela Siljo.

HOW TO PURIFY BUTTER
HERBED BUTTER

NIT'IR QIBE

UTENSILS: large, deep cooking pot (8 quart) large, covered container strainer

INGREDIENTS:

12 lbs.	butter
2 large	fresh ginger (chopped)
1 medium	fresh garlic (chopped)
1 large	red onion (chopped)
1 tbsp.	fenugreek (*abish*)
2 tsp.	white cumin (*azmud*)
3 tsp.	sacred basil (*besobila*)
1 tsp.	cardamom seeds
1 Tbsp.	oregano
1/2 tsp.	turmeric

PREPARATION: Wash and chop *red onion, garlic* and *ginger* together, rinse together, and set aside. Melt all the *butter* in the pot over low heat and stir, making sure the color does not change. Skim the foam from the top of the mixture as it cooks, until there is no more foam. Add blended onion, garlic, and ginger and *spices* to the butter and continue simmering, stirring gently for 15 minutes. Remove from heat and let stand until the spices settle. Strain into a large container, cover and store in a cool place. Use as needed.

Nit'ir Qibe is a basic ingredient in the preparation of authentic, tasteful Ethiopian dishes. It is used to prepare all dishes requiring butter.

5

DRIED, POWDERED INJERA

DIRQOSH

UTENSILS: large plastic bag or covered container

INGREDIENTS: 3-6   fresh injeras

PREPARATION: Dry *injeras* in warm oven. Break into small pieces or pound to a powder as desired. Store in covered container or large bag at room temperature.

Dirqosh is used as substitute for fresh injera. It is added to ready-made stew and left in the pot to soak up the sauce, then served hot.

ETHIOPIAN MUSTARD

SENAFICH'

UTENSILS: medium mixing bowl
mortar and pestle

INGREDIENTS: 2 cups   mustard seeds
3 Tbsp.   oil
1 cup   water
to taste   salt

PREPARATION: Using mortar and pestle pound *mustard seeds* to powder. Add 1 cup *water*, 3 Tbsp. *oil* and *salt* to taste. Mix well till mixture is slightly liquid.

Refrigerate and keep in closed container.

Senafich' is similar to English mustard. It is very popular during Lent.

FALSE BANANA INSET
(ENSETE EDULE HORAN MUSACEAE)

QOCH'O

UTENSILS: two deep containers (crockery or stainless steel bowl at least 8-10″ deep)
scraping utensil
pounding utensils

INGREDIENTS:

5 lbs.	False banana stem below ground level	
5 lbs.	False banana stem above ground level	

PREPARATION: Cut the *stem (below ground level)* into strips and scrape with a sharp scraper. Then lay the strips on a slanting board which is placed over a bowl to collect qoch'o scrapings. Squeeze *qoch'o* scrapings, making sure all the juices are collected into the deep container. Set aside. Pound the 5 lb. *underground part of the stem* separately and place on top of the qoch'o. Cover and allow to ferment for fifteen days. After fifteen days, open and mix the qoch'o thoroughly. Then cover again and let it stand for another fifteen days for further fermentation. Keep in a cool dry place. Use as needed.

Qoch'o is one of the ancient food plants. There are different varieties of false banana. The quality of food varies according to the varieties of the plant. Qoch'o can be used to make injera, alcohol, or t'ella. Qoch'o also can be chopped into small pieces and cooked with meat and cabbage.

8

HOW TO PREPARE FENUGREEK

ABISH

UTENSILS: medium frying pan
small covered container
mortar and pestle
grinder
large cloth

INGREDIENTS: 1 1/2 cup   fenugreek seeds
(Trigonella foenum graecum)
(L. Papilionaceae)
2 1/4 cup   red onions

PREPARATION: Wash *fenugreek* seeds in cold water and spread on a clean cloth to dry. In a medium pan, roast the dried fenugreek seeds. Mix the fenugreek and *onions* together and pound using mortar and pestle. Let stand overnight, spread out on a clean cloth again to dry. When completely dry gring to a fine powder and sift. Store in a covered container and use as needed.

Abish is used to spice red pepper and various other dishes. It is also whipped with ice cold water to make a refreshing drink.

GERMINATED GRAINS

BIQIL

UTENSILS: Large mixing bowl with cover
large tray
mortar and pestle or electric grinder
sieve
large covered container

INGREDIENTS: 2 cups   barley, wheat, sorghum, corn,
broad beans

PREPARATION: In a large mixing bowl soak *wheat, barley, sorghum, corn* and *broad beans*. Cover and let stand overnight. The next day, discard water and let the soaked cereals stand for three to five days. Spread over a large tray, set in the sun to dry, or put in a light oven. When dry pound into flour. Sift through a sieve and store in a clean tight covered container.

Biqil preparation takes a minimum of three to four days. When preparing food that needs *Biqil* the time to prepare it, should be taken into consideration.

GREEN PEPPER PASTE

T'IQUR QARYA AWAZE

UTENSILS: medium frying pan
medium mixing bowl
glass jar with lid
mortar and pestle

INGREDIENTS:

2 cups	green pepper
1/2 Tbsp.	garlic
1/2 Tbsp.	ginger
1/4 tsp.	bishop's weed
1/4 tsp.	false cardamom
1/2 tsp.	sacred basil
3 cups	water (cold)

PREPARATION: Fry *green pepper* in a pan until it is well done. Add into a bowl of cold water and stir. Drain the water and dry the pepper in the sun or in the oven (low heat 30-40 minutes). Chop pepper and pound gently. Add *spices* gradually and pound everything together. Store in glass jar and refrigerate to keep fresh. Yields 6 to 8 servings.

T'iqur Qarya Awaze can be served as a dip with injera, bread, meat, etc.

RED PEPPER (CHILI)
(CAPSICUM FRUTESCENS
C. ABYSSINICUM)

BERBERE

UTENSILS:
large mixing bowl
medium frying pan
mortar and pestle
covered container or jar

INGREDIENTS:

15 lbs.	red pepper (dried new Mexican chilie)
5 lbs.	garlic (fresh)
5 lbs.	ginger roots (fresh)
2 cups	red onions (chopped)
1 lb.	rue seed
1 cup	sacred basil
1/4 cup	cloves
1/4 cup	cinnamon
1/4 cup	cardamom
1 cup	bishop weed
1 1/2 cup	salt
3 cups	water

PREPARATION: Remove all the seeds from the *red peppers* and wash the peppers several times. Dry in the sun or in a moderate oven until crisp and then pound lightly. Pound the *garlic, ginger, red onion, rue seed, sacred basil* and *bishop weed* together. Mix spice mixture with 3 cups of *water*, add to the red pepper and blend well. Cover tightly and let stand for 12 hours. Dry the mixture again in the sun or in a moderate oven. In the meantime, heat the *cinnamon, salt, cardamom* and *dried cloves*. Add to the above mixture and grind together to a fine powder. Store in a tight container. Use as needed.

Berbere is a basic ingredient in the preparation of Ethiopian dishes. It is used to prepare all dishes requiring berbere.

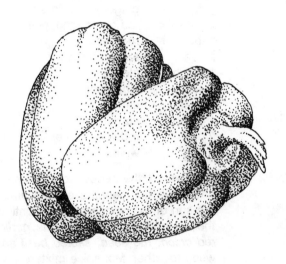

Green pepper

RED PEPPER PASTE

AWAZE

UTENSILS: large mixing bowl
medium frying pan
mortar and pestle
covered container or jar

INGREDIENTS:

15 lbs.	red pepper (New Mexican chilies)
5 lbs.	garlic (fresh)
5 lbs.	ginger roots (fresh)
2 cups	red onion (chopped)
1 lb.	rue seed
1 cup	sacred basil
1/4 cup	cloves
1/4 cup	cinnamon
to taste	salt
1/4 cup	cardamom
2 cups	red wine or *t'ej*
1 cup	water

PREPARATION: Remove all the seeds from the *red peppers* and wash the peppers several times. Dry in the sun or in a moderate oven until crisp and then pound lightly. Pound the *garlic, ginger, red onion, rue seed, sacred basil* and *bishop weed* together. Mix spice mixture with *2 cups* of *wine* and *1 cup* of *water*, add *red pepper* and blend well. Cover tightly and let stand for 12 hours. Spread the mixture again in the sun or in the oven to dry. In the meantime, heat the *cinnamon, salt, cardamom*, and dried *cloves*. Add to the above mixture and ground together to a fine powder.

Boil a little garlic and onion. Drain and mash. Add cold water. Strain the mixture and use the

14

water to mix with the red pepper in part. Put in
a tightly covered container and refrigerate.
Another way of making the paste is to use 3
cups of red wine or *te'j* only and no water.

Awaze is used to give flavor to raw meat or certain mild sauces.

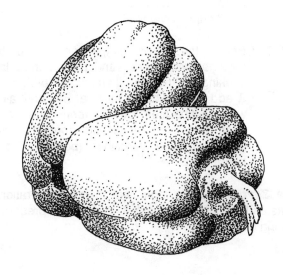

Green pepper

SPICED OIL

YETENET'TERE ZEYT

UTENSILS: mortar and pestle
large cooking pan
large covered container or bottle
sieve

INGREDIENTS:
3 1/2 cups	oil
3 tsp.	garlic (chopped)
1 1/2 tsp.	ginger (chopped)
3 tsp.	onion (chopped)
3 tsp.	basil dry
3 1/2 cups	water

PREPARATION: Pound the *garlic*, *ginger*, *onion* and *basil together* with mortar and pestle. In a large cooking pot mix the oil and water, bring to boil & add the powdered mixture. Boil until all the water evaporates. Cool to room temperature, strain through a sieve and store in a clean tightly covered container (bottle). Use as needed.

Yetenet'tere Zeyt is a basic ingredient in the preparation of authentic, tasteful Ethiopian dishes. It is used to prepare all dishes requiring oil.

HOW TO PREPARE SPICED POWDERED PEPPER SEEDS

AFRINJ

UTENSILS: medium mixing bowl
                    large cloth
                    mortar and pestle
                    covered container or glass jar
                    sifter

INGREDIENTS: 2 cups   red pepper seeds (fresh, peeled,
                                  and chopped)
                  1/2 cup   ginger (fresh, peeled,
                                  and chopped)
                  1/2 cup   garlic (fresh, peeled,
                                  and chopped)
                  1/2 cup   red onions (fresh, peeled,
                                  and chopped)
                  1 Tbsp.   black pepper
                  to taste   salt

PREPARATION: Sift and wash *red pepper seeds* and spread
out on a clean cloth to dry. Mix dried red pepper seeds with the rest of the ingredients, except salt, and pound well. Spread out again to
dry. Add the *salt* and grind to a fine powder.
Put powder in a clean covered container.

Afrinj is used to spice raw beef.

HOW TO PREPARE SPICED, HOT, POWDERED PEAS

MIT'IN SHIRO

UTENSILS:
large cooking pot
large mixing bowl
large frying pan
mortar and pestle
covered container, preferably glass

INGREDIENTS:

11 cups	peas
5 cups	lentils
5 cups	chick peas
5 cups	beans
5 cups	red pepper (*berbere*)
1 cup	garlic (fresh, chopped)
1 cup	ginger (fresh, chopped)
1 cup	red onions (fresh, chopped)
1 cup	rue seeds
1 cup	oregano
2 Tbsp.	fenugreek
1 cup	sacred basil
15 pods	cardamom seeds
2 Tbsp.	cloves
2 Tbsp.	cinnamon
1 Tbsp.	bishop's weed
1 Tbsp.	coriander
to taste	salt
2 cups	water, wine or t'ej

PREPARATION: Wash the *peas, lentils, chick peas*, and *beans* separately, boil in water for 3-5 minutes and drain. Place in a low oven for a while and before they are dry, roast separately. Grind to remove seeds from pods and discard the burnt seeds. Set aside. Take the fresh *ginger, garlic,* *onion, rue* and *oregano* and pound together until fine. Mix powdered spices with 2 cups of *water*, red *wine* or *t'ej*. Add red pepper to the mixture and pound lightly together. Then put in a large bowl, cover and leave overnight. The next morning, spread the mixture out on a clean mat in the sun to dry. You can also dry this in a very low oven. In a frying pan roast the *sacred basil, fenugreek, coriander, cloves, cinnamon, salt* and *bishop's weed* over a low fire for about 3 minutes and add to the above. Grind together to a fine powder. Store in a dry place, in a tightly closed container. May be kept indefinitely. Use in small amounts as needed.

Mit'in Shiro is a ready mixed powdered legume spice used to make an instant hot sauce or is added to regular w'et to give it a thicker consistency.

Peas

VERY HOT RED PEPPER
(BIRDS-EYE-CHILI, C. MINIMUM)

MIT'MIT'A

UTENSILS: large mixing bowl
medium frying pan
mortar and pestle
covered container or jar

INGREDIENTS:

10 lbs.	red pepper (serrano)
1/4 cup	cardamom
2 Tbsp.	cloves
1 cup	salt

PREPARATION: Dry *chilies* in the sun or moderate oven until crisp and then pound lightly. Heat the *cloves*, *salt*, and *cardamom* separately. Mix with the chili mixture and grind together to fine powder. Use as needed. Store in tight container or jar.

Mit'mit'a is made from the *smallest* and *hottest* of the chilies. It is used when eating raw meat.

Green pepper (serano)

MILDLY SPICED POWDERED PEAS

NECH' SHIRO

UTENSILS: large cooking pot
large frying pan
mortar and pestle
covered container (preferably glass)

INGREDIENTS:

11 cups	peas
5 cups	beans
5 cups	chick peas
1 cup	sacred basil
1/2 cup	bishop's weed
1 cup	ginger (chopped)
1 cup	garlic (chopped)
1/2 cup	false cardamom
1 cup	oregano
1/4 cup	fenugreek
1 cup	red onion (chopped)
to taste	salt

PREPARATION: Wash the *beans, peas* and *chick peas* separately. Put in boiling water for 30 minutes. Place in a low oven for a while. Before they are dry, roast and set aside. Grind to remove the seeds from pods and discard the burned seeds. Set aside. Pound the *ginger, garlic* and *onion* together. Place the mixture in low oven to dry. Heat all the *spices* in a frying pan and mix with the beans and peas. Grind the mixture into a fine powder and sift. Store in a covered container in a dry place and use in small amounts as needed.

Nech' Shiro is used to make a curry sauce. It is mixed with water, salt and *injera* is added to make a "shiro (*fitfit*)." Also, when washing chicken, it is rubbed on the skin and lightly grazed with flame to remove feather roots.

Appetizers

There is a wide range of snacks both for children taken between meals and by adults at coffee time. Some of these are also carried by travelers in their journeys because they keep very well.

Qolo, ch'ikko, beso, dabbo qolo and *qwant'a* are excellent examples of these.

BARLEY MEAL

BESSO

UTENSILS: medium mixing bowl
strainer

INGREDIENTS:

1 lb.	barley flour
1/2 lb.	butter (spiced)
1 Tbsp.	red pepper (*berbere*) or red pepper paste (*awaze*)
to taste	salt
1 cup	boiling water
1/2 tsp.	false cardamom

PREPARATION: See recipe for barley flour. Prepare the barley flour. Pour boiling *water* into a bowl and add *butter*, red pepper or *red pepper paste, salt* and *false cardamom*. Mix well. Add *barley flour* a little at a time and mix well to avoid lumps. Keep adding flour until dough is thick and dry and ready to serve. 6-8 servings.

Variation: For a somewhat sweeter version of besso, substitute honey (about 2-3 tbsp.) for the salt in the recipe and leave out the red pepper paste.

Besso is an instant meal. Will last several days without refrigeration. May be served as a snack.

BOILED WHEAT CEREAL

YESINDE NIFRO

UTENSILS: medium cooking pot
                   covered container or jar

INGREDIENTS: 1 lb.   wheat cereal
                   4 cups   water
                   to taste   salt

PREPARATION: In a medium pot boil the *wheat* cereal in *water*
                   and some *salt*. Cook covered over medium
                   heat until cereal is soft and done (15-20 min-
                   utes). Drain water and serve hot cereal in a
                   bowl or individual bowls. Makes 6 or more
                   servings. Refrigerate unused cereal.

Nifro is a common name for all boiled cereals: *wheat, barley, corn, lentils, chick peas*, etc. The cereals can be boiled sepa-rately or mixed. It may be eaten as a whole meal by elders who only eat grain cereals during periods of fasting.

COLLARD GREEN MIXED IN SPICED COTTAGE CHEESE

AYIB BE GOMEN

UTENSILS: medium cooking pan
covered container

INGREDIENTS: 1 lb.   collard green
1 lb.   cottage cheese
1 tsp.   black pepper
3 Tbsp.   butter
to taste   salt

PREPARATION: Wash the *collard green* in running water and chop. Boil the collard green in 6 cups of *water* for 5-10 minutes. Discard the water and set aside. Add 1 tsp. *black pepper*, 3 Tbsp. *butter* and mix with *cottage cheese*. Add the chopped collard green and mix well with the cottage cheese. Makes 6 servings. Refrigerate to store.

Ayeb be Gomen makes a tasty dish with bread or injera. It is always served as side dish with Kitfo.

COTTAGE CHEESE MIXED WITH VERY HOT RED PEPPER & SPICED BUTTER

AYIB BEMIT'MIT'A

UTENSILS: small mixing bowl

INGREDIENTS: 1 lb.   cottage cheese
1/4 tsp.   black pepper
2 Tbsp.   butter (spiced)
as needed   salt
1 tsp.   very hot red pepper
(*mit'mit'a*) (Birds-Eye-
Chili) (c. minimum)

PREPARATION: Mix *cottage cheese, black pepper, butter, salt*
and *mit'mit'a* in the mixing bowl. Serve cold or
hot. Makes 4-6 servings. Refrigerate to store.

Ayib Bemit'mit'a is a delicious side order eaten with all kinds of
meal.

CRUSHED PAN BREAD
IN SPICED BUTTER

CHE'CHE'BSA

UTENSILS: heavy skillet, 12 inches
large mixing bowl
sifter

INGREDIENTS;

1 lb.	wheat flour
2 cups	butter (spiced)
1/4 tsp.	false cardamom
1/4 cup	red pepper
to taste	salt
1-2 cups	water

PREPARATION: Sift the 1 lb. *flour* and *salt* into a large bowl. Adding *water*, a little at a time, knead well. Lightly grease heavy skillet or griddle. Shape dough like pizza in pan 1/2 inch thick. Cook slowly on both sides until golden and crisp. Take out and break into small pieces and mix with *butter, false cardamom* and *red pepper*. Serve hot or cold. Makes 5-6 servings. To store refrigerate.

Che'che'bsa is eaten by itself as a breakfast food or snack.

DRIED FISH

YEASSA QWANT'A

UTENSILS: glass jar or plastic bag
dehydrater
cloth
covered container or plastic bags

INGREDIENTS:

10 lbs.	fish fillet
to taste	salt
2 Tbsp.	red pepper paste (awaze)
1 Tbsp.	lemon juice

PREPERATION: Remove bones from the *fillets* and cut into long strips. Mix salt, red pepper paste (*awaze*), *black pepper* and *lemon juice* together. Pour over the fish strips and toss until evenly coated. Dehydrate meat or hang fish until completley dry (4 - 5 days). Break dried fish into smaller pieces and serve raw or fried.

Yeassa Qwant'a is mainly a snack food served on special occasions such as during a fasting period. It is very versatile and can be consumed as it is, fried, cooked in a sauce, or ground to powder and stewed. (**Ye'assa Minchet Abish**)

DRIED MEAT

QWANT'A

UTENSILS: glass jar or plastic bag
dehydrater
cloth
covered container or plastic bags

INGREDIENTS:

10 lbs.	beef or lamb
to taste	salt
1 Tbsp.	black pepper
1 cup	red pepper (*berbere*) or red pepper paste (*awaze*)

PREPARATION: Trim excess fat from *meat* and wipe meat with clean cloth. Cut meat into long strips. Mix *salt, black pepper* and *red pepper (berbere) or red pepper paste (awaze) (optional)* and rub on strips of meat. Dehydrate meat. Break dried meat into smaller pieces and serve raw or fried. Store in closed jar or plastic bags to keep fresh and crisp indefinitely. Makes 4-6 servings.

Qwant'a is mainly a snack food served on all occasions, especially with cocktails. It is very versatile and can be consumed as it is, fried, cooked in sauce or ground to powder and put in shiro, etc.

DRIED MEAT WITH SPICED BARLEY MEAL

YEQWANT'A CHI'KKO

UTENSILS: medium cooking pan
covered container

INGREDIENTS:
1 lb.	barley flour
2 cups	dried meat (qwanta)
1 tsp.	red pepper (*berbere*)
1 tsp.	ginger (powder)
1/2 tsp.	cardamom
1/4 tsp.	black cumin
3 cups	butter
to taste	salt

PREPARATION: Melt the *butter* and add all of the *spices*. Pound dried meat into fine powder and sift. Add *red pepper* to the powdered meat. Make a paste by mixing the *barley flour* with the melted butter and dried meat mixture. Mix thoroughly and set aside to cool. When cool and dry, cut into small one inch squares and serve. Store covered in cool place. Makes 6-8 servings.

Yeqwant'a Chi'kko is ch'ikko mixed with dried meat. It is served for snacks or as appetizers.

DRIED GREEN COFFEE BEANS

BUNNA QELA

UTENSILS: medium size frying pan
medium mixing bowl (2-4 qt.)
covered container (1-2 qt. size)

INGREDIENTS:
1 lb.	Dried green coffee beans
2 cups	butter (spiced)
to taste	salt

PREPARATION: Roast the *dried green coffee beans* in low fire. Set aside. Melt *butter* and add *salt* to taste. Mix roasted dried green coffee beans evenly. Store in clean covered container. Makes 3-4 servings.

Bunna Qela is dried green coffee beans roasted and then mixed with spiced butter. It is usually eaten when hot coffee is not available.

ETHIOPIAN PIZZA

ANNEBABERO

UTENSILS: medium mixing bowl
medium pizza pan
small bowl

INGREDIENTS:

2 lbs.	wheat flour
1 tsp.	baking powder
to taste	salt
1 Tbsp.	red pepper (*berbere*) or red pepper paste (*awaze*)
1 cup	butter or oil
4 cups	water (lukewarm)

PREPARATION: Add *wheat flour* to lukewarm *water* and rub with your fingers to form a pancake-like mix. Add *baking powder* and *salt*, mix well. Spread in a round pizza pan and bake over a low heat for 50 minutes; remove and set aside. Make a second crust of the same size and in the same way. Before the second crust is well-done, pour some of the *butter* (about 1/2 cup) on it, spread and put the first crust on top (like a sandwich). Repeat this process until you run out of the first cup of the butter. In a small bowl, mix remaining butter or *oil* with *red pepper* and spread lightly over the hot crusts. Make sure that both sides are spread evenly. Cut in small squares or pizza slices to serve. Should make about 4 Annebaberos. Cover and store in a cool place. Serve hot or cold.

Annebabero is a delicious snack or appetizer.

FRIED INJERA,
LIGHTLY BUTTERED AND SPICED

QATEGNA

UTENSILS: large frying pan
medium mixing bowl

INGREDIENTS: 4-6 pieces   injeras
1/2 cup   red pepper (*berbere*)
1 cup   butter
1 lb.   minced beef (optional)

PREPARATION: Mix *red pepper* and *butter* together. Bake *injeras* over a low heat in a pan. Spread the above mixture over the injera until completely covered. Roll the injera and cut into four or leave it open and cut into 2-inch squares. Serve hot. Refrigerate to store but better eaten while it is still fresh and hot.

Qategna is also a snack and an appetizer but it may be served for breakfast as well.

*Qategna can also be served with *minced beef* mixed with red pepper and butter. It becomes a light meal by itself.

ROASTED WHEAT CEREAL MIXED IN SPICED BUTTER

QORI

UTENSILS: medium size frying pan
small mixing bowl
spatula
covered container or jar

INGREDIENTS: 1 lb.   wheat cereal
1/2 cup   butter (spiced)

PREPARATION: Over medium heat, roast *wheat* cereal in a pan turning over with a spatula so each side is evenly cooked. When crisp and golden pour cereal into bowl. Melt *spiced butter* and pour into the bowl that contains the cereal. Mix well and serve cold. Makes 6 servings. Store in refrigerator.

Qori is roasted wheat cereal mixed in spiced butter, excellent for snacks.

ROASTED WHEAT CEREAL

YESINDE QOLO

UTENSILS: medium size frying pan
spatula
covered container or jar

INGREDIENTS: 1 lb.   wheat cereal

PREPARATION: Over medium heat, roast *wheat* cereal in a pan turning over with a spatula so each side is evenly cooked. When crisp and golden turn out onto a plate and serve hot or cold. Store in a covered container or jar. Makes 6 servings.

Qolo is a common name for all roasted cereals: *wheat, barley, sorghum*, etc. They are good for snacks.

SAMBOSSA PASTRY

UTENSILS:	medium skillet
	blender
	sifter
	covered container

Pastry:

INGREDIENTS:	1 1/2 lbs.	all purpose flour, sifted
	to taste	salt
	1 cup	margarine
	1	egg
	1 tsp.	vinegar
	5 Tbsp.	cold water
	3 cups	vegetable oil (for cooking)

PREPARATION: Sift *flour* and *salt* together. Blend the *margarine* until mixture resembles cornmeal in texture. Beat *egg, vinegar* and *water* together. Add to flour and salt mixture. Mix thoroughly and shape into a ball. On a lightly floured surface, roll out the dough in a circle a few inches in diameter. Using a small knife, cut the circle in half. Dip a finger in water and moisten the straight edge. Then shape each semi-circle into a cone.

Filling:

| UTENSILS: | heavy sauce pan |

INGREDIENTS:	1/2 cup	red onions (finely chopped)
	1 lb.	lean ground (lamb or beef)
	1/2 tsp.	ground ginger or minced ginger
	1/2 tsp.	turmeric
	1/2 tsp.	garlic powder or 1 garlic clove, minced

1/2 tsp.	cayenne pepper or 1 green chili pepper, diced
to taste	salt
1/2 tsp.	cinnamon
4 sprigs	fresh coriander chopped (optional)
3 sprigs	fresh mint chopped
2 cups	water

PREPARATION: Combine all ingredients in heavy sauce pan. Bring to boil and stir to keep smooth. Reduce heat to medium and let mixture simmer uncovered. Correct flavour for spices and salt balance. As water simmers away, stir often to prevent mixtures from sticking, especially during final stages. Cook until all the liquid evaporates. If ground meat has a lot of fat, drain off at this point. Let the mixture cool slightly before stuffing. (Leftover filling makes a tasty sandwich.)

Holding the cone in one hand, fill it with 1 1/2 to 2 tsps. of the Sambossa filling. Moisten and press the top edge of the cone to close. Pour 3 cups of the vegetable oil in a heavy skillet and heat until oil sputters. Fry the Sambossas, several at a time, until golden brown on both sides. Place the golden brown Sambossas on thick paper towels to rid excessive oil. Serve hot or cold with or without chutney. Serving 6-8.

Sambossa is a delicious appetizer. Crisp and tasty.

SPICED BARLEY MEAL

CHI'KKO

UTENSILS: medium cooking pan
2 inch deep container

INGREDIENTS: 1 lb.   barley flour
3 cups   butter
1 tsp.   cardamom
to taste   salt
1/4 tsp.   black pepper
1/4 tsp.   cloves
1/2 tsp.   red pepper (*berbere*)

PREPARATION: Melt the *butter* and add all of the *spices*. Make a paste by mixing the *barley flour* with the melted butter. Put mixture in a deep container and allow to cool. Cut into small pieces before serving. Store in a cool place. Makes 6-8 servings.

Chi'kko may be served with tea, coffee, as a snack or with cocktails as an appetizer.

SPICED BARLEY MEAL MIXED WITH HONEY

CHI'KKO BEMAR

UTENSILS: deep container
covered container

INGREDIENTS: 4 cups   barley flour
6 cups   pure honey

PREPARATION: Put *barley flour* in a deep bowl. Make a paste by mixing the barley flour with the 6 cups of *honey*. Put mixture in a deep container and allow to settle. Cut in small pieces before serving. Store in a cool place. Makes 4-6 servings.

Chi'kko Bemar is barley flour mixed with honey and not with butter. It is very delicious. In time of long trip it can be diluted with water to supplement food and consumed in a liquid form.

SPICED BEEF JERKY

WAT'ELA

UTENSILS: mixing bowl (medium)
covered container
dehydrater

INGREDIENTS:

2 lbs.	beef
2 Tbsp.	red pepper (*berbere*)
to taste	salt
1 tsp.	black pepper
1/2 tsp.	cardamom
1 Tbsp.	wine or *t'ej*

PREPARATION: Cut *meat* into thin wide slices and pound. Mix *all the ingredients* in bowl. Coat the sliced meat with the mixture. Dehydrate the meat. To serve: cut the Wat'ela in small pieces or fried crisp. Store in clean, covered container.

Wat'ela is a delicacy served as a snack or as an appetizer.

42

SPICED SAUSAGE

QWALIMA

UTENSILS: medium mixing bowl
dehydrater
covered container

INGREDIENTS:

1 lb.	ground beef chopped
1/2 lb.	intestine (beef or lamb)
1 cup	butter (spiced)
1/4 tsp.	garlic powder
1/4 tsp.	false cardamom
1/4 tsp.	ginger
to taste	salt

PREPARATION: In the mixing bowl add the *ground beef, butter, garlic powder, false cardamom, ginger, black pepper* and *salt*. Blend well. Clean *intestine* in running water thoroughly. Stuff the mixture into the intestine and tie into small sausages.

Dehydrate the sausages to dry. When dry cut sausages in small pieces and serve raw or fried. Store in closed jar or plastic container to keep fresh and crisp indefinitely. Makes 4-6 servings.

Qwalima is a snack served on special occasions. It is very versatile and can be consumed as it is, fried or cooked.

TOASTED SORGHUM

YEMASHILA ABEBA

UTENSILS: medium size cooking pan
medium size frying pan
spatula
covered container or jar

INGREDIENTS: 1 lb   sorghum seeds

PREPARATION: Boil the *sorghum* in enough water for 10 minutes. Drain & discard the water. Roast sorghum in a pan turning over with spatula so each side is evenly cooked. When crisp, turn out onto a plate and serve hot or cold. Store in a covered container or jar. Makes 6 servings.

Yemashila Abeba, unlike other Qolo, is boiled before roasted. It is served as a snack with coffee or tea.

WHEAT NUTS OR SNACKS

DABBO QOLO

UTENSILS: medium mixing bowl
deep frying pan
scissors
covered container or jar

INGREDIENTS:

1 lb.	wheat flour
1 cup	cooking oil
2 Tbsp.	sugar
to taste	salt
2 cups	water

PREPARATION: Put *wheat flour, sugar, salt* in a bowl and mix thoroughly, adding *water* a little at a time. Knead until the dough is a thick, smooth paste. Add sugar or salt and oil. Knead for 15 more minutes. Roll into thin strips, 1/4 inch thick, and cut into tiny pieces with scissors. Deep-fry in boiling *oil* until crisp and brown. Serve hot or cold. Store in covered container indefinitely. Serves 6-12.

Dabbo Qolo is a snack food that may also be served as an appetizer with cocktails.

*For variation, add a little red pepper while kneading or food coloring as desired.

Beverages
(Alcoholic)

Alcoholic beverages are made at home for domestic consumption, and special types - a variety of *t'ej* - for festive occasions.

T'ella is the most popular. *Katikala* , a drink akin to Schnaps, is also common in many parts of the country.

BANANA FLAVORED HONEY WINE

YEMUZ T'EJ

UTENSILS: small wooden barrel (3 gal. capacity)
earthenware or large glass container
medium cooking pot

INGREDIENTS:

1 1/2 cups	woody hops (*Gesho*) (Rhamnus phinoides L'Herit Rhamnaceae)
32 oz.	honey
1 gallon	water
6 medium	bananas

PREPARATION: Mix *honey* with *water* and put into a deep container. Store for 3 days in a warm room. Set aside. In a medium pot, cook the *hops* in 6 cups of honey water. Bring to boil and simmer over a low heat for 15 minutes to avoid the bitter taste. Put boiled hops honey water in air tight container and let stand for 5 days. When mixture ferments, remove hops using strainer and cover again for 24 hours. On the next day peel and slice *bananas*, add to the mixture and let stand for 7 days in air tight container. Before serving filter through clean cloth. Store in a cool room or bottle and refrigerate.

Taste for sweetness, add more hops to the mixture and cover in air tight container for 2-3 days. If too bitter add 1 cup honey and cover with air tight container for another 20 days. Serves 6-12.

Yemuz T'ej is also another version of t'ej with a slightly different color and flavor. It can be served on different occasions. This is also an alcoholic beverage.

CITRON FLAVORED HONEY WINE

YETRINGO T'EJ

UTENSILS: small wooden barrel (3 gallon capacity)
earthenware or large glass container
medium cooking pot
strainer

INGREDIENTS:

1 1/2 cups	woody hops (*Gesho*) (Rhamnus phinoides L'Herit Rhamnaceae)
32 oz.	honey
1 gallon	water
1 medium	citron (*tringo*) (*cedrat*)

PREPARATION: Mix *honey* with *water* and put into a deep tight container. Store for 3 days in a warm room. Set aside. Take 6 cups of the honey water and put in the medium cooking pot with the *woody hops*. Bring to boil and simmer over a low heat for 15 minutes to avoid the bitter taste. Put boiled hops and honey water aside to cool and add to the remaining honey water mixture and let it stand 5 days. When mixture ferments, remove hops using strainer and add the sliced peeled seedless *citron* into the *t'ej*. Cover container again for 15-20 days. Remove the citron, cover again and store in a cool place or put into bottles after filtering. Refrigerate. Serves 6-12.

Taste for sweetness add more hops to the mixture and cover with air tight container for 2-3 days. If too bitter add 1 cup honey and cover with air tight container for another 20 days.

Yetringo t'ej can be served with any meal at any time of the day. This also is an alcoholic beverage.

COFFEE FLAVORED HONEY WINE

YEBUNNA T'EJ

UTENSILS: small wooden barrel (3 gal. capacity)
earthenware or large container
medium cooking pot
strainer
cheese cloth

INGREDIENTS:

1 1/2 cups	woody hops (*Gesho*) (Rhamnus phinoides L'Herit Rhamnaceae)
32 oz.	honey
1 gallon	water
1 lb.	coffee beans

PREPARATION: Mix *honey* with *water* and put into a deep container. Store for 3 days in warm room. Set aside. Take 6 cups of the honey water and put in the medium cooking pot with the woody hops. Bring to boil and simmer over a low heat for 15 minutes to avoid the bitter taste. Put boiled hops and honey water aside to cool and add to the remaining honey water mixture and let it stand for 5 days. When mixture ferments remove hops using strainer and cover again for 24 hours.

Roast *coffee beans*, cool, and grind. Tie ground coffee in a clean cheese cloth and dip it into the mixture, let stand for 15-20 days in air tight container. Before serving filter through clean cloth. Store in a cold place or bottle and refrigerate.

Taste for sweetness, add more hops to the mixture and cover in air tight container for 2-3 days. If too bitter add 1 cup of honey and cover with air tight container for another 20 days. Serves 6-12.

Yebunna T'ej is a very tasty, alcoholic drink. Excellent for parties or at meal time.

To give coffee flavored wine the coffee colour, boil coffee and add to the honey water and stir.

ETHIOPIAN VODKA

KATIKALA

UTENSILS: 3 large clay pot 6 gallon capacity
1 large container with cover
medium frying pan
sieve

INGREDIENTS:

2 cups	barley flour (qitta preparation)
5 cups	red sorghum flour
7 cups	corn flour
7 cups	millet flour
7 cups	red t'ef flour
5 cups	wheat flour
10 cups	germinated wheat flour
3 cups	pounded hop leaves (Gesho) (Rhamnus phinoides L'Herit Rhamnaceae)

PREPARATION:
I. In a large clay pot mix the *germinated wheat* flour the *hop leaves* and 5 cups of water together. Cover and let stand for 3 days. In a large container mix the *sorghum flour, corn flour, millet flour, t'ef flour* and *wheat flour* with 2 gallons of *water*. Cover and let stand for 3 days.

II. Qitta:- Add 2 cups of *barley flour* in a small container with 1 1/2 cups of water. Mix well. Sift a little of the flour over a working table and spread to coat evenly. Add the dough and pat lightly with oiled hands into a circle about 1 - 1 1/2 cm thick. Bake the qitta for 10 minutes. Bake other side of qitta for another 10 minutes. While baking qitta make sure it is covered. When ready brush away the excess flour. Add the hot qitta and the remaining germinated wheat flour to the clay pot. Add 4 1/2 gallons of water, cover and let stand for four to five days. After the five days pour the katikala mixture through a sieve into another clay pot. Distill the liquid. Store in a glass container. Use as needed.

Katikala can be made from honey using same recipe. The alcohol content is 37.9% by volume. It is very intoxicating and is a favorite drink in most rural areas.

* In most beverage preparation smoking the clay pot is practiced for it gives a special odor to the containers. Different dried plants such as 'wiera' sticks (dea africana) and 'tengyt' (otoslegia integrifolia) are used to smoke tela pot.
To smoke a clay pot or a calabash, first thoroughly wash and drain the containers. Then invert the container over a smoking fire of some dried plants. Smoke the container until the sides and the bottom are quite warm.

ETHIOPIAN BEER

T'ELLA

UTENSILS: small wooden barrel (3 gallon)
earthenware or large glass container
medium frying pan

INGREDIENTS:

3 lbs.	woody hops (*Gesho*) finely ground (Rhamnus phinoides L'herit Rhamnaceae)
1 1/2 gallon	water
3 lbs.	barley, finger millet (ground grain malt)
1 lb.	wheat

PREPARATION: Separate the *hop*-leaves from the wood. Grind them and mix with 1 gallon of *water*. Cover the wooden barrel with the mixture and set aside.

Biqil: Germinated *wheat*. Soak *wheat* in water for three days. When the wheat starts to germinate place it in a deep fastened container covered for three days. On the third day take out the mixture and dry it in the sun or in a slow oven until dry and grind it well, and place in the wooden barrel with the other mixture. Put this in a wooden barrel with the other mixtures.

Asharo: Roasted ground grain. Roast *barley, finger millet* until golden brown. Pound to remove husks. Discard the husks and grind to fine powder. Mix flour with a little water until smooth and bake for 5-7 minutes in low heat. Let it cool. Break the bread into small pieces and put into the above container with the other mixtures. Add remaining finely ground hop leaves. Cover the wooden barrel with a clean cloth and allow the mixture to settle for eight hours. After the mixture has settled, add the remaining water and seal the wooden barrel for 7-9 days. Before serving filter through clean cloth. Store container in a cold room or bottle and refrigerate. Serves 6-12.

If *T'ella* is consumed before three days, it is called *Gush T'ella*. T'ella is a refreshing, mild alcoholic drink served at all times.

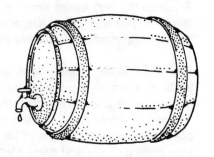

GINGER FLAVORED HONEY WINE

YEZINJIBIL T'EJ

UTENSILS: small wooden barrel
earthenware or large glass container
medium cooking pot
strainer

INGREDIENTS:

1 1/2 cups	woody hops (*Gesho*) (Rhamnus phinoides L'Herit Rhamnaceae)
32 oz.	honey
1 gallon	water
4 medium	fresh ginger

PREPARATION: Mix *honey* and *water* and put into a deep tight container. Store for 3 days in a warm room. Set aside. Take 6 cups of the mixture of honey and water and put in the medium cooking pot with the *woody hops*. Bring to boil and simmer over a low heat for 15 minutes to avoid the bitter taste. Put boiled hops and honeywater aside to cool and add to the remaining honey and water mixture and let it stand for 5 days. When mixture ferments remove hops using strainer and cover again for 24 hours. On the next day, wash and peel *ginger* and cut into big pieces and then add to the mixture. Let stand for 15-20 days in air tight container. Before serving filter through clean cloth. Store in a cool place or bottle and refrigerate. Serves 6-12.

Taste or sweetness add more hops to the mixture and cover with air tight container for 2-3 days. If too bitter add 1 cup honey and cover with air tight container for about another 20 days.

Yezinjibil t'ej is an alcoholic drink served on special occasions or with meals.

Ginger

HYDROMEL OR HONEY WINE

T'EJ

UTENSILS: small wooden barrel
earthenware or large glass container
medium cooking pot strainer

INGREDIENTS: 1 1/2 cups   woody hops (*Gesho*) (Rhamnus phinoides L'Herit Rhamnaceae)
32 oz.   honey
1 gallon   water

PREPARATION: Mix *honey* with *water* and put in a deep container. Store for 3 days in a warm room. Set aside. In a medium pot cook the *hops* taking 6 cups of honey and water mixture. Bring to boil and simmer over a low heat for 15 minutes to avoid the bitter taste and let cool. Add boiled hops and honey water to the remaining honey water mixture and let it stand for 5 days.

When mixture ferments, remove hops using strainer and cover again for 24 hours. Taste for sweetness, add more hops to the mixture and cover with air tight container for 2-3 days. If too bitter add 1 cup honey and cover with air tight container for about 20 days. Before serving filter through clean cloth. Store container in a cold room or bottle and refrigerate. Usually after 4-8 days the *t'ej* becomes strong and sediment collects at the bottom of the container. Pour out slowly. Served chilled or at room temperature. Serves 6-12.

T'ej is a honey wine that can be served with any meal. It is an alcoholic beverage.

ORANGE FLAVORED HONEY WINE

YEBIRTUKAN T'EJ

UTENSILS: small wooden barrel (3 gal. capacity)
earthenware or large glass container
medium cooking pot
strainer

INGREDIENTS:

1 1/2 cups	woody hops (*Gesho*) (Rhamnus phinoides L'Herit Rhamnaceae)
32 oz.	honey
1 gallon	water
7 medium	orange peels

PREPARATION: Mix *honey* with *water* and put into a deep container. Store for 3 days in a warm room. Set aside. On the third day squeeze out the wax like residual from the liquid. Take 6 cups of honey water and put in the medium cooking pot with the *woody hops*. Bring to boil and simmer over a low heat for 15 minutes to avoid the bitter taste. Put boiled hops and honey water mixture aside to cool and add to the remaining honey water mixture and let it stand 5 days. When mixture ferments remove hops using strainer and add the sliced orange peels into the t'ej. Cover container again for 15-20 days. Remove the peels, cover again and store in a cool place or put into bottles after filtering.

Taste for sweetness, add more hops to the mixture and cover with air tight container for 2-3 days. If too bitter add 1 cup honey and cover with air tight container for another 20 days. Serves 6-12.

Yebirtukan T'ej is a refreshing alcoholic beverage with an orange flavor.

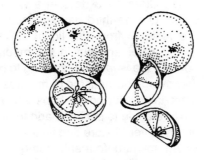

Oranges

PRUNE FLAVORED HONEY WINE

YEPRUN T'EJ

UTENSILS: small wooden barrel (3 gal. capacity)
earthenware or large glass container
medium cooking pot
strainer

INGREDIENTS:

1 1/2 cups	woody hops (*Gesho*) (Rhamnus phinoides L'Herit Rhamnaceae)
32 oz.	honey
1 gallon	water
3 lbs.	ripe prunes

PREPARATION: Mix *honey* and *water* and put into a deep container. Store for 3 days in a warm room. Set aside. On the third day squeeze out the wax like residual from the liquid. Take 6 cups of honey water and put in the medium cooking pot with the *woody hops*. Bring to boil and simmer over a low heat for 15 minutes to avoid the bitter taste. Put boiled hops and honey water mixture aside to cool and add to the remaining honey water mixture and let it stand for 5 days. When mixture ferments remove hops using strainer and add the seedless *prunes* into the t'ej. Cover container again for 15-20 days. Remove the prunes, cover again and store in a cool place or put into bottles after filtering.
Taste for sweetness, add more hops to the mixture and cover with air tight container for 2-3 days. If too bitter add 1 cup honey and cover with air tight container for another 20 days. Serves 6-12.

Yeprun T'ej is a refreshing alcoholic beverage with a slight taste of prune.

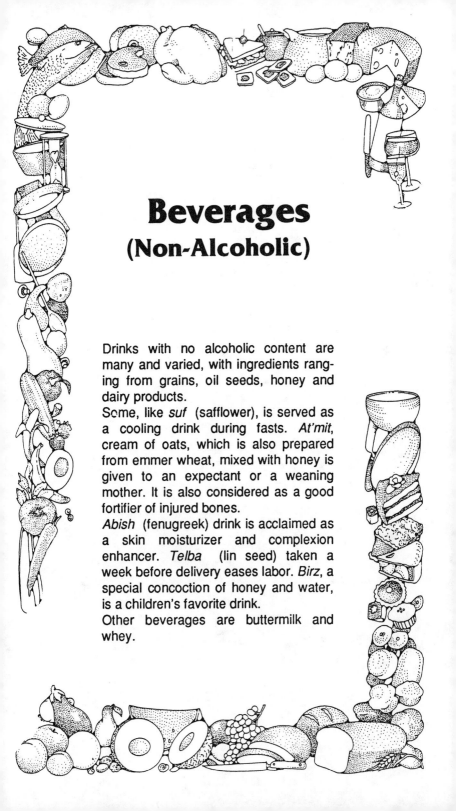

Beverages
(Non-Alcoholic)

Drinks with no alcoholic content are many and varied, with ingredients ranging from grains, oil seeds, honey and dairy products.

Some, like *suf* (safflower), is served as a cooling drink during fasts. *At'mit*, cream of oats, which is also prepared from emmer wheat, mixed with honey is given to an expectant or a weaning mother. It is also considered as a good fortifier of injured bones.

Abish (fenugreek) drink is acclaimed as a skin moisturizer and complexion enhancer. *Telba* (lin seed) taken a week before delivery eases labor. *Birz*, a special concoction of honey and water, is a children's favorite drink.

Other beverages are buttermilk and whey.

BARLEY GRUEL

YEGEBS AT'MIT

UTENSILS: medium mixing bowl
medium cooking pot

INGREDIENTS:

1 cup	barley flour
2 1/2 cups	water (cold)
2 1/2 cups	water (boiling)
3 Tbsp.	sugar or honey

PREPARATION: Put barley flour in mixing bowl and add 2 1/2 cups of cold *water* stirring slowly. Add and stir mixture into 2-1/2 cups of boiling water. Add, *sugar* or *honey* and cook for 8-10 minutes stirring constantly. Serve hot.

Gruel is highly popular among mothers after delivery, convalescents, and small children. Gruel can also be prepared from any other cereal using the same procedure. When used as a weaning food for children it is highly recommended to mix some legumes in the form of flour.

COFFEE

BUNNA

UTENSILS: frying pan
coffee grinder
coffee pot

INGREDIENTS:

1 cup	coffee beans
1 tsp	cloves
1/4 tsp	cinnamon
7 cups	water

PREPARATION: Roast the *coffee beans* in a hot frying pan until golden brown. In the coffee grinder add the roasted *coffee*, *cloves* & *cinnamon* and grind to fine powder. Bring the 7 cups of water to boil add the ground spiced coffee and boil for 5 minutes. Serve coffee in a small coffee cup.

Bunna, Ethiopian Coffee is world wide known for its aroma, flavor and satisfaction. Coffee is usually drunk for breakfast, after lunch, and in the afternoon. In most household coffee drinking has a ritual beyond explanation.

CREAM OF OATS

YE'AJJA AT'MIT

UTENSILS: medium mixing bowl
medium cooking pot

INGREDIENTS: 1 cup   oats
2 cups   water
to taste   sugar or honey
1 Tbsp.   butter (optional)

PREPARATION: Soak the *oats* in *water* overnight. The next day, rub the oats between the fingers to completely remove the husks. Strain and boil the liquid while stirring. When it thickens add *sugar* or *honey* to taste and serve hot in cups. Makes two servings. *Butter* added before serving gives it a rich, creamy consistency.

Ye'ajja at'mit is a thick, delicious drink which can be taken any time. This, like the cereal butter is highly recommended for pregnant as well as new mothers. Ye'ajja At'mit tastes better when served fresh from the pot.

Oats

FENUGREEK WITH HONEY

ABISH BE MAR

UTENSILS: medium mixing bowl
blender

INGREDIENTS: 1 cup   fenugreek powder
3 1/2 cups   water
1/2 cup   honey

PREPARATION: In a medium mixing bowl, mix the fenugreek and water. Cover and let stand overnight. The next day discard the water and beat the fenugreek until it becomes light and fluffy. Add the honey and beat until it is well blended. Serve cold.

Abish be Mar is frequented mainly by ladies. It is believed to enhance the complexion.

HOT BREW MADE FROM COFFEE LEAVES

QUT'I

UTENSILS: tea pot for brewing or serving

INGREDIENTS: 2 Tbsp.   coffee leaves
               6 cups   water
               to taste   sugar

PREPARATION: Dry *coffee leaves* in the sun or put in low oven. Boil coffee leaves in 6 cups of *water*. When water starts turning reddish brown in color remove leaves and serve hot. Add *sugar*, cream or honey to taste. Makes about 6 servings. Store remaining coffee leaves in a covered jar.

Qut'i is a close substitute for tea.

Tea pot

69

HONEY MIXED WITH WATER

BIRZ

UTENSILS: jug or 1 quart bottle (glass or plastic)

INGREDIENTS: 1/2 cup   pure honey
                  6 cups   soda or plain water

PREPARATION: Put 1/2 cup *honey* into a jug or bottle. Add 6 cups of *water* or *soda water* stirring to dissolve completely. Leave for two days at room temperature. Refrigerate or add ice to the jug before serving. Makes about 6 servings. Keep refrigerated.

Birz is a honey drink that is very popular. It is very refreshing and considered very healthy.

Honey comb

REFRESHING DRINK MADE FROM FLAX

TELBA

UTENSILS: medium roasting pan
medium mixing bowl
medium pitcher
sifter

INGREDIENTS: 1 cup   flax seeds
6 cups   water
2 tsp.   sugar or honey

PREPARATION: Roast *flax seeds* in pan at low heat for 5-10 minutes. Prevent from burning. Remove from heat and let cool. Pound roasted flax to fine powder. Sift into medium bowl. Add *water* and stir. Let stand until the liquid separates from the powder. Strain and pour liquid into pitcher. Add *sugar* or *honey* to the liquid to taste. Refrigerate. Serve cold. Yields 4-6 servings. Flax powder should be stored in closed jar.

Telba is a light refreshing drink. The liquid can be mixed with Injera to make Telba Fitfit. Telba is mildly laxative.

Flax

REFRESHING DRINK MADE FROM SUNFLOWER SEEDS

SUFF

UTENSILS: medium cooking pot
strainer
medium bowl
blender
medium pitcher

INGREDIENTS: 2 cups   sunflower seeds
8-12 cups   water
to taste   sugar or honey
a few sprigs rue

PREPARATION: Boil *sunflower seeds* at high temperature in 6 cups of *water* for 15 minutes. Remove from heat and drain off liquid. Grind seeds in blender until they turn to a paste. Put paste in medium bowl and add 6 cups of cold water. Mix, strain, pour liquid in jar and refrigerate. Discard the paste. Serve cold with a sprig of *rue*. Add *sugar* or *honey* to taste. Makes 4-6 drinks. Store in refrigerator.

Suff is a delicious, refreshing drink consumed primarily during Lent or fasting. The liquid can be mixed with Injera to make Yesuff Fitfit.

Sunflower

Traditional Bread

Injera is fermented, sour pancake-like. It is made from *t'ef*, barley, corn, wheat, millet, sorghum flours or a combination of two or more of them.

Great care must be made when preparing traditional *injera* . Pure water must be used to make *injera* since the additives in tap water destroy *t'ef* yeast. If your tap water contains only chlorine, boil it in an open pot for five minutes to remove the chlorine, and then let cool. In a hot muggy weather decrease fermentation time. In Cold temperature, increase fermentation time.

The use of forks and spoons is precluded with *injera* - the bread is torn into pieces and used to scoop up the other foods in the meal.

INJERA MADE FROM BARLEY

YEGEBS INJERA

UTENSILS: large pancake pan
deep mixing bowl

INGREDIENTS:

1 1/2 lbs.	barley flour
1 pkt.	yeast
6 cups	water

PREPARATION: Mix *barley flour* by hand in 2-3 cups *water* making sure the mixture is not too liquid. Cover and leave over night. The next day mix with 3 cups of warm *water* till mixture becomes thin. If mixture does not rise add 1 packet of *yeast* or baking powder and leave for 10-15 minutes. Preheat pancake pan at 420°. Take 3/4 cup of the mixture and pour into the pan slowly, starting at the edge going clockwise in circles and coming to the center. Let it stay for 2-4 minutes. When ready the rim of the injera will rise from the pan. Remove immediately and place on a clean cloth to cool. Cover and store in a cool place or refrigerate 2-3 days. Makes 6-8 servings.

Yegebs injera unlike t'ef injera is slightly thick. It is served with all kinds of dishes on any occasion.

INJERA MADE FROM CORN

YEBEQOLO INJERA

UTENSILS: large pancake pan or large frying pan
deep mixing bowl

INGREDIENTS: 1 1/2 lbs.   corn flour
6 cups   water
1 pkt.   yeast

PREPARATION: Mix *corn flour* with 6 cups of *water* till it is thin. Add 1 packet *yeast* and mix well. Keep till mixture rises.

Preheat pancake pan at 420°. Take 3/4 cup of the mixture and pour into the pan slowly, starting at the edge, going clockwise in circles and coming to the center. Let it stay for 3-4 minutes. When ready the rim of the corn injera will rise from the pan. Remove immediately and place on a clean cloth to cool. Corn injera can be covered and stored in a cool place or refrigerated for about 2-3 days. Makes 6-8 servings.

Yebeqolo injera unlike t'ef injera is slightly thick. It is served with all kinds of dishes on any occasion.

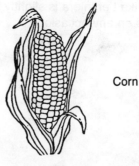

Corn

BREAD MADE FROM MILLET

YEDAGUSSA INJERA

UTENSILS: large pancake pan
                   deep mixing bowl

INGREDIENTS: 1 1/2 lbs.   millet flour
                   1 pkt.   yeast
                   6 cups   water

PREPARATION: Mix *millet flour* by hand in 2-3 cups water making sure the mixture is not too liquid. Add 1 pkt of *yeast* and mix well. Cover and let stand till mixture rises. Preheat pancake pan at 420°. Take 3/4 cup of the mixture and pour into the pan slowly starting at the edge, going clockwise in circles and coming to the center. Let it stand for 3-4 minutes. When ready the rim of the millet injera will rise from the pan. Remove immediately and place on a clean cloth to cool. Millet injera can be covered and stored in cool place or refrigerated for about 2-3 days. Makes 6-8 servings.

Yedagussa Injera, unlike t'ef injera, is slightly thick. It is served with all kind of dishes on any occasion.

INJERA MADE FROM RICE

YERUZ INJERA

UTENSILS: large pancake pan or large frying pan
deep mixing bowl

INGREDIENTS:
1 1/2 lbs.	rice flour
1 pkt.	yeast
6 cups	water

PREPARATION: Mix *rice flour* with 6 cups *water* till the mixture is thin. Add 1 packet of *yeast* and mix well. Keep till mixture rises. Preheat pancake pan at 420°. Take 3/4 cup of the mixture and pour into the pan slowly, starting at the edge, going clockwise in circles and coming to the center. Let it stay for 2-4 minutes. When ready the rim of the rice injera will rise from the pan. Remove immediately and place on a clean cloth to cool. Rice injera can be covered and stored in a cool place or refrigerated for about 2-3 days. Makes 6-8 servings.

Yeruz injera unlike all the injeras is white in colour and slightly thick. It is served on special occasions.

INJERA MADE FROM T'EF

YET'EF INJERA

UTENSILS: large pancake pan or large frying pan
large pot
deep mixing bowl

INGREDIENTS: 1 1/2 lbs.   t'ef flour (not available
in the U.S.) (Eragrostis
Abyssinica)
6 cups   water
2 pkt.   yeast

PREPARATION: Clean *t'ef* thoroughly by removing all foreign
materials. Grind to a fine powder. Sift into a
deep mixing bowl. Adding water gradually and
rubbing with the fingers to avoid lumps, make
the flour into a dough.

In a large pot dissolve *yeast* in warm water and
add the flour mixture and mix. Leave covered
for 2-3 days until fermentation begins and water rises to the top. Carefully discard the water.
Boil 2 cups of water. Take 1 cup of the mixture,
put in the boiling water (Abseet'). Place on a
warm stove and stir continuously until it becomes thick. Cool and pour back into the original pot. Add more water, cover and let stand till
the mixture rises.

Preheat pancake pan at 420°. Take 3/4 cup of
the mixture and pour into the pan slowly, starting at the edge, going clockwise, in circles
and coming to the center. Cover pan 2-4 minutes. When ready, the rim of the injera will rise
from the pan. Remove immediately and place
on a clean cloth to cool. Injera can be covered

and stored in a cool place or refrigerated for about 2-3 days. Makes 6-8 servings.

Yet'ef injera is a soft, spongy, sour bread made from a rye like grain called t'ef which is grown in Ethiopia. A staple food, it is served with all kinds of dishes on any occasion and eaten with the fingers, and is usually served cold.

INJERA MADE FROM SORGHUM

YEMASHILA INJERA

UTENSILS: large pancake pan or medium frying pan
deep mixing bowl

INGREDIENTS:

1 1/2 lbs.	sorghum flour
1 pkt.	yeast
6 cups	water

PREPARATION: Mix *sorghum flour* with 6 cups of *water* till the mixture is thin. Add 1 packet *yeast* and mix well. Keep till mixture rises.

Preheat pancake pan at 420°. Take 3/4 cup of the mixture and pour into the pan slowly, starting at the edge, going clockwise, in circles and coming to the center. Let it stay for 3-4 minutes. When ready the rim of the sorghum injera will rise from the pan. Remove immediately and place on a clean cloth to cool. Sorghum injera can be covered and stored in a cool place or refrigerated for about 2-3 days. Makes 6-8 servings.

Yemashila injera unlike all injeras is slightly thick. It is served with all kinds of dishes on any occasion.

INJERA MADE FROM WHEAT

YESINDE INJERA

UTENSILS: large pancake pan or large frying pan
large mixing bowl

INGREDIENTS: 1 1/2 lbs.   flour (self-rising)
6 cups   water

PREPARATION: Mix *self-rising flour* with 6 cups of *water* till the mixture is thin. Preheat pancake pan at 420°. Take 3/4 cup of the mixture and pour into the pan slowly starting at the edge, going clockwise in circles and coming to the center. Let it stay for 3-4 minutes. When ready the rim of the injera will rise from the pan. Remove immediately and place on a clean cloth to cool. Wheat injera can be covered and stored in a cool place or refrigerated for 2-3 days. Makes 6-8 servings.

Yesinde injera is served with all kinds of dishes on any occasion.

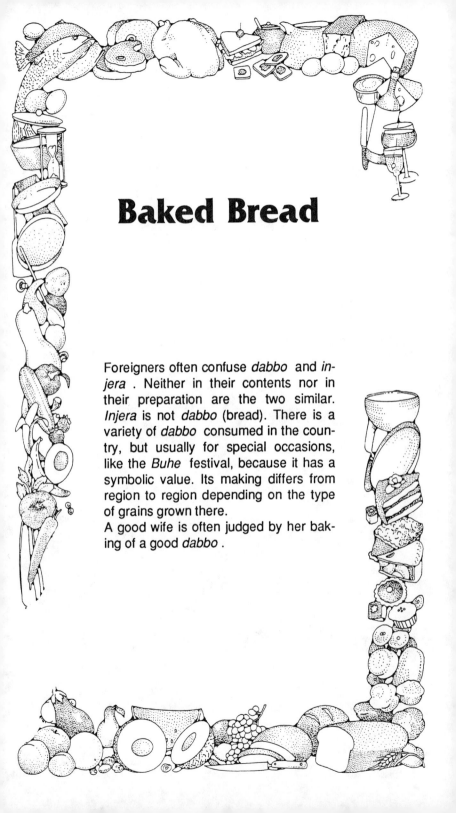

Baked Bread

Foreigners often confuse *dabbo* and *injera* . Neither in their contents nor in their preparation are the two similar. *Injera* is not *dabbo* (bread). There is a variety of *dabbo* consumed in the country, but usually for special occasions, like the *Buhe* festival, because it has a symbolic value. Its making differs from region to region depending on the type of grains grown there.

A good wife is often judged by her baking of a good *dabbo* .

BARLEY BREAD (UNFREMENTED)

GOGO (YEGEBS DABBO)

UTENSILS: medium mixing bowl
baking pan (medium)
blender
Aluminium foil

INGREDIENTS: 1 lb   barley flour (sifted)
to taste   salt
1 1/2 cup water

PREPARATION: Add the *barley flour* into a medium mixing bowl. Stir in the water a little at a time. Knead for three minutes. Sprinkle a little flour on the baking pan. With a slightly oiled palm turn the dough on the baking pan and pat into a circle about 1-1/2 cm thick. Cover with foil and bake for 40 to 45 minutes. When ready, brush away excessive flour and serve. Store in a covered container. Makes 4 - 6 servings.

Gogo is a light bread, tasty with any food.

BARLEY BALLS

T'IHLO

UTENSILS: mixing bowl
closed container

INGREDIENTS: 2 lbs.   barley flour
3 cups   water (boiling)

PREPARATION: Add 3 cups of boiling *water* to the *barley* powder, mix well and make into balls by hand.
These balls, *t'ihlo*, may be eaten plain and/or
dipped into a ready made we't (stew). This will
make about 1/2 dozen small balls. They may
be stored in a covered container and refrigerated.

T'ihlo may be served as a snack when eaten plain or a meal
when dipped in we't.

Barley balls

BREAD MADE WITH SPICED MINCED BEEF SAUCE

YEMINCHET ABISH DABBO

UTENSILS: medium mixing bowl
deep baking pan (medium)
medium cooking pot

INGREDIENTS:

1 tsp.	baking powder
3 lbs.	semolina flour
2 pkt.	yeast
1/2 tsp.	garlic (fresh)
1/2 tsp.	ginger (fresh)
to taste	salt
1/2 lb.	minced meat (beef)
1 cup	red onions (chopped)
1 cup	red pepper (*awaze* or *berbere*)
1 lb.	butter
1/4 Tbsp.	cinnamon
1/4 Tbsp.	false cardamom
3 cups	water (warm)

PREPARATION: *Dough*: Dissolve 2 packets *yeast* in 1/2 cup warm *water*, mix and let stand for 1 hour. When yeast starts to dissolve add 3 lbs. *semolina* and knead using the remaining warm water a little at a time. Cover with wax paper and keep overnight at room temperature.

Sauce: Cook *onions* until golden brown. Add *butter and salt*. Stir. Add *red pepper*. Add *minced beef* and cook at medium heat for 30 minutes. Add *ginger, garlic, false cardamom* and *cinnamon*. Mix well. Remove from heat when water content cooks out. Divide dough in 3 equal parts. Mix the two parts with grease from the top of the sauce and knead in well. The leftover dough is mixed with the minced beef sauce. Spread 1/2 dough, mixed with grease, at bottom of pan. Spread dough, mixed with minced beef sauce on top. Spread remaining half dough mixed with grease on the very top. Place in 335° oven and bake for 1 hour. When done, crust turns golden brown. Serve hot or cold. Makes 6 or more servings. Store covered in refrigerator.

Yeminchet abish dabbo is a delicious bread, a meal in itself. It is especially made for festive occasions, dinners, cocktails, etc.

BREAD MADE WITH SPICED MINCED FISH SAUCE

YE'ASSA DABBO

UTENSILS: medium mixing bowl
medium baking pan
medium cooking pan

INGREDIENTS:

1-2 tsp.	baking powder
3 lbs.	semolina flour
2 pkt.	yeast
3-4	fish fillets (boneless)
1 cup	red onions (chopped)
1/2 cup	cooking oil
1/2 tsp.	garlic (fresh)
1/2 tsp.	ginger (fresh)
1/4 tsp.	black pepper
as needed	salt
1/2 cup	t'ej or red cooking wine
3 cups	water
1/3 cup	red pepper (*berbere*) or red pepper paste (*awaze*)

PREPARATION: *Dough*—Dissolve 2 packets *yeast* in 1/2 cup of lukewarm *water*. Combine *semolina*, 2 tsp. *baking powder* and yeast mixture in 2 1/2 cups of water and knead. Cover with wax paper and keep overnight at room temperature. Add 1 Tbsp. *oil* and mix just before baking.

Fish Sauce—Cook *onions* in remaining oil until golden brown. Add 1 cup of water and stir. Add 1/3 cup *red pepper* (berbere or awaze) and cook for 1/2 hour. Cut *fish* into cubes or thin strips and add to cooking pan when liquid has evaporated. Add *t'ej* or *wine, ginger, black pep-*

89

per, garlic and simmer sauce over low fire, cover for 10 minutes. Remove from heat and cool.

Mix the grease that is on top of the sauce with the dough. Divide dough into two equal portions. Spread one-half of the dough into a baking pan bottom and sides. Pour fish sauce over the dough. Spread remaining dough over the sauce and put pan in oven. Bake for 1 hour at 335°. Take out when golden brown and serve hot or cold. Keep covered with foil. Serves 6-8.

Ye'assa dabbo, like all other breads baked with meat sauces, is very festive, made only on special occasions.

CHICK PEA BREAD (FERMENTED)

YESHIMBRA DABBO

UTENSILS: 2 medium mixing bowl
baking pan
blender
aluminum foil

INGREDIENTS: 1 lb   chickpea flour sifted
1 pkt   yeast
to taste   salt
2 cups   water (warm)

PREPARATION: Mix 1/2 lb of *chick pea flour* with 1 pkt *yeast* in 1 cup of water in a medium mixing bowl. Cover and keep overnight. Add the remaining 1/2 lb of *chick pea* flour in 1 cup of *water* and knead well. Cover and let dough stand for 1 hour. Sprinkle a little flour on the baking pan. With a slightly oiled palm turn the dough on to the baking pan and pat into a circle about 1 to 1-1/2 cm thick. Bake at 335° oven for 40 to 45 minutes. Be sure to cover with foil when baking. When ready brush away any excess flour and serve. Cover and refrigerate to store. Makes 4-6 servings.

Yeshimbra Dabbo is a tasty bread especially prepared for parties.

Baked Bread

CHICK PEA PIZZA

YESHIMBRA DABBE

UTENSILS: medium frying pan
medium mixing bowl

INGREDIENTS:
2 cups	chick pea flour
1 Tbsp.	oil
1/2 tsp.	red pepper (*berbere*)
2 cups	water
to taste	salt

PREPARATION: Blend chick pea powder in two cups of *water*. Add *salt, oil, red pepper (berbere)* and mix well. When mixture becomes slightly thick pour on the frying pan. Remove when chick pea mixture is cooked. Serves 6. Refrigerate.

Yeshimbra Dabbe is another version of chick pea bread. It is soft and delicious.

CHICKEN BREAD

YEDORO DABBO

UTENSILS: large mixing bowl
deep baking pan (medium)

INGREDIENTS:

3 lbs.	wheat flour
2 pkt.	yeast
1 tsp.	sugar
4 cups	hot water
1/4 tsp.	bishop's weed
1 lb.	butter or margarine
1 cup	red onion (chopped)
1/3 cup	red pepper (*berbere*) or red pepper paste (*awaze*)
2 pieces	boneless chicken thighs
1/4 tsp.	cloves
1/4 tsp.	false cardamom
1/4 tsp.	ginger
1/4 tsp.	garlic
4 boiled	eggs

PREPARATION: *Chicken Sauce*—Brown *onions* in medium frying pan on very low heat. Cut *chicken* into cubes and add to the onions along with *butter*. Stirring occasionally, add *red pepper* (or awaze). Add *spices: bishop's weed, cloves, false cardamom, ginger* and *garlic* and simmer for about 10-15 minutes. Remove from the heat and set aside. Boil eggs, peel, and set aside.

Dough—Add *yeast, sugar* and 1 cup of *flour* to 4 cups of *hot water* in a large mixing bowl. Rub between fingers until yeast and sugar dissolve. Add remaining flour and keep rubbing until a soft dough is formed. Set aside for a

93

few seconds until it rises. Skim a small amount of grease from the top of the chicken sauce and add half of the skimmed grease to the dough, still rubbing with fingers. Put half of the dough into a baking pan. Spread all of the sauce with the boiled eggs on top of the dough. Put the remaining dough on top. Let the dough rise to the rim of the pan. Place the pan in 350° pre-heated oven. Bake for 20-30 minutes checking until crisp and brown. Remove from oven and spread top the remaining half of the skimmed chicken sauce grease. Serve hot. Do not use a knife when cutting, but break with fingers. To store, cover and refrigerate. To serve the remaining warm in a medium pre-heated oven for 3-4 minutes. Serves 6-8.

Yedoro Dabbo is a tasty bread especially prepared for parties.

DECORATED PAN BREAD

AMBASHA (HIMBASHA)

UTENSILS: medium mixing bowl
medium baking pan

INGREDIENTS:

1 lb.	whole wheat flour
1/2 cup	cooking oil
1 tsp.	cumin
1 pkt.	yeast
2-3 cups	water
to taste	salt

PREPARATION: Dissolve *yeast* in 2 cups of lukewarm water, mix and put aside until dissolves. Add the following ingredients into the dissolved yeast: 1 lb. *whole wheat flour*, 1/2 cup *oil, salt & cumin*. Knead well and cover for 2 hours. Knead some more and cover for 1 hour. Spread out dough in slightly greased baking pan and decorate using forks. Put in 335° oven and bake for 30-60 minutes. Serve hot or cold. Makes 6 or more servings. Store in covered container.

Ambasha (Himbasha) is a light, tasty bread. It may be eaten plain or with butter.

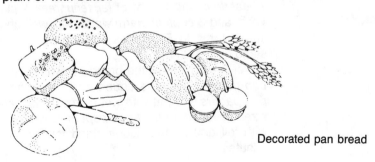

Decorated pan bread

EMMER WHEAT BREAD

YEAJJA DABBO

UTENSILS: large mixing bowl
large baking pan
sheet pan paper
aluminum foil

INGREDIENTS:
2 cups	germinated wheat (split)
1/4 tsp.	bishop's weed
1/4 tsp.	cardamom
1/4 tsp.	coriander
1/4 tsp.	garlic (mashed)
1/4 tsp.	ginger (mashed)
1/4 tsp.	onion (mashed)
5 lbs.	emmerwheat flour (sifted)
to taste	salt
4 cups	tej
1/4 tsp.	fenugreek
2 pkt.	yeast
6 cups	water (warm)

PREPARATION: Mix *germinated wheat*, *bishop's weed*, *cardamom*, *coriander*, *onion*, *garlic* with 2 cups of *tej*, and 2 cups of *warm water* together in a large container. Cover and leave for 3 days. After the 3 days, add the *emmer wheat flour*, *salt*, 2 cups of *tej*, *fenugreek*, 2 pkt *yeast* and 3 cups of warm water. Mix well and knead for 4 to 5 minutes and let the dough stand for 2-1/2 hours.

Cover the bottom of the bread pan with *sheet pan* papers, pour the dough on to the *sheet pan_papers* and pat with wet palms to desired size. Cover with *sheet pan papers*. Cover pan with foil and let the dough stand for 8 to 10 minutes.

Place the baking pan in 350° preheated oven. Bake for 45 minutes. When bread feels firm to the touch, remove. Serve hot or cold. Makes 6 or more servings. Store in covered container.

Yeajja Dabbo is a wholesome and delicious bread.

STEAMED LIGHT BREAD

HIBIST

UTENSILS: medium mixing bowl
large steamer pan

INGREDIENTS:

2 lbs.	all purpose flour
3 pkt.	yeast
1 tsp.	bishop's weed
1/4 tsp.	nutmeg
1/2 cup	oil (cooking)
3 1/2 cups	water
to taste	salt

PREPARATION: Dissolve *yeast* 1/2 cup of warm *water*. Add 2 lbs. *all purpose flour* in 3 cups of water. Add *bishop's weed, nutmeg*, and 1/2 cup *oil* and knead. Cover and leave overnight at room temperature. Knead again the next day. Pour into steamer pan and decorate by hand. Keep water boiling over low heat to steam bread 3 hours or while wooden pick inserted in center comes out clean. Serve hot or cold. Makes 6-8 servings. Store covered, refrigerate or at room temperature.

Hibist is a nice light bread, tasty with any food. Serve with tea or we't (stew).

WHOLE WHEAT BREAD

YE'ABESHA DABBO

UTENSILS: medium mixing bowl
deep baking pan
small frying pan
covered container (bread bin)

INGREDIENTS:

3 pkt.	yeast
1 tsp.	sugar
3 lbs.	self-rising flour
1 cup	cooking oil
1 Tbsp.	bishop's weed
1/2 Tbsp.	ginger powder
1/2 Tbsp.	garlic powder
4 cups	water (warm)

PREPARATION: Mix *yeast*, 1 1/2 cups *flour* and *sugar* with 3 cups warm *water* until the mixture looks like pancake mix. Cover with a piece of cloth for about 1/2 hour until it rises. Add remaining flour and 1 cup water and knead well. Cover again for about 15 minutes until it rises.

Add *bishop's weed, ginger* and *garlic* with the dough; cover for about 15 minutes until it rises again. Pour into a bread pan and bake in preheated oven, at 350° for an hour or until golden. Serve hot or cold. Store in a plastic bag or in bread bin to keep it soft and fresh. Cut in sizes desired. Serves 6-8.

Ye'abesha Dabbo can be eaten plain, with butter for a snack, at breakfast or tea time.

99

WHOLE WHEAT BROWN BREAD

T'IQUR SINDE DABBO

UTENSILS: medium mixing bowl
deep baking pan (medium)

INGREDIENTS:

3 pkt.	yeast
1 lb.	brown self-rising flour
2 tsp.	baking powder
2 lbs.	whole wheat flour
1 cup	oil
1 tsp.	ginger powder
1/2 tsp.	garlic powder
1/2 tsp.	cardamom
2 tsp.	black cumin
4 cups	water
to taste	salt

PREPARATION: Dissolve 1 1/2 packets *yeast* in 1/2 cup of warm *water*. Add *ginger, garlic, cardamom, black cumin, salt* and 3 Tbsp. *self-rising flour*. Stir, cover and let stand overnight at room temperature. The next day dissolve the remaining 1 1/2 packets of yeast in 3 1/2 cups of warm water and add 2 tsp. *baking powder, 2 lbs. whole wheat flour, oil*, and the remaining self-rising flour. Knead well and set aside for about 1 hour. Place in baking pan. Bake at 335° oven for an hour. Serve hot or cold. Store covered. Serves 6-8.

T'igur Sinde Dabbo is a wholesome and delicious bread, good any time of day with any food.

Meat Dishes
(Beef and Lamb)

In the highland regions, *injera* (the staple bread and its variable companion, *we't* make up the standard dish of the population.

We't may be made from meat, poultry, legumes, vegetables, eggs or fish. Its preparation differs from place to place and from house to house. Thus, the recipes in this book are based on what is commonly practiced. Cooking time has been reduced to a minimum for practical purposes, but also to avoid loss due to overcooking of vitamin C, especially in vegetables.

And increasing or decreasing the amount of *berbere* determines a hot or mild stew.

BEEF COOKED IN RED PEPPER

AWAZE MEREQ

UTENSILS: medium cooking pan
small mixing bowl

INGREDIENTS: 2 cups   red onions (chopped)
1 cup   red pepper paste (*awaze*)
1/4 tsp.   garlic powder
1/2 tsp.   ginger powder
1 1/2 lbs.   meat with bone (beef)
4 cups   water
1 1/2 cups   butter (spiced)
to taste   salt

PREPARATION: Cook *red onions* without grease in medium pan until golden brown. Wash and cut *meat* into small pieces and add to the pan, with the *bone*, and cook until tender. Add *water*. Add *ginger* and *garlic* and stir well. Mix *awaze* and *butter* in a small bowl and add to the meat. Stir gently. Add *salt* and serve hot. Makes 6 servings. Refrigerate to store.

Awaze Mereq is a mild, tasty stew eaten with pieces of injera added.

BOILED BEEF

GINTIR

UTENSILS: medium cooking pot

INGREDIENTS:
1 cup	red onions (chopped)
1 cup	butter (spiced)
1 1/2 lbs.	meat and ribs (beef or lamb)
1/2 tsp.	ginger (paste fresh)
1/4 tsp.	black pepper
to taste	salt
2 cups	water

PREPARATION: Cook *onions* without grease in a low heat making sure the color does not change. Add the *meat* and stir well. Add *butter* and cook till meat is brown. Add water and mix well. Put in the *spices* and simmer for 30 minutes till gravy thickens. Serve hot. Makes about 6 servings. Store in refrigerator.

Gintir is a light meal usually served for brunch.

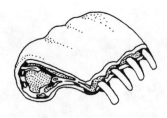

Ribs

DRIED BEEF STEW

YEQWANT'A ZILBO

UTENSILS: 2 medium cooking pots

INGREDIENTS: 1 lb.   qwanta (dried beef)
                 2 cups   red onions (chopped)
                 1/2 tsp.   funugreek
                 1/2 cup   red pepper (*berbere*)
                 1 cup   butter (spiced)
                 1/2 cup   t'ej or red wine
                 1 cup   shiro water (*shiro kerera*)
                 3 cups   water
                 to taste   salt

PREPARATION:
I.   Brown *onions* in a pan. Add *fenugreek* and stir making sure the onion doesn't burn by adding a little *water* at a time (1 cup). Add *red pepper* and *butter*. Put in *t'ej* or *wine* and stir again.

PREPARATION:
II.   In another pan add the *dried beef* in 2 cups water and boil until it is soft. Remove the boiled beef and add to the onion mixture. Discard water.

PREPARATION:
III.   In a small bowl dissolve "shiro" in water. Stir and let it stand for 5 minutes till the shiro rest on to the bottom.Add the *shiro water* or *"kerera"* to the beef and onion mixture. Add salt as needed. Stir and simmer over low heat for 20-30 minutes. When stew thickens it is ready to serve. Makes 6 servings. May be stored in refrigerator.

Yeqwant'a Zilbo makes a nice main course for daily consumption, especially when fresh meat is not available. Serve with injera preferably.

FRIED BEEF STEW

T'IBS WE'T

UTENSILS: medium frying pan (10-12 inches)
medium cooking pot

INGREDIENTS:

2 cups	red onions (chopped)
2 cups	butter (spiced)
1 cup	red pepper (*berbere*)
2 lbs.	beef (cut into cubes)
1/2 tsp.	cardamom
1/2 tsp.	ginger
1/4 tsp.	black cumin
1/4 tsp.	cloves
1/4 tsp.	garlic
1/4 tsp.	black pepper
1/2 cup	t'ej or red wine
2 cups	water
to taste	salt

PREPARATION: Cook *onions* without grease until they turn brownish red color. Add *butter* and stir. Add *berbere* and *wine* or *t'ej* stirring gently.

In a medium pan, fry the *beef* separately, without grease, until it is tender. Add the fried meat to the cooking onions and stir gently. Add water and keep stirring. Add all the *spices* and *salt* and let the sauce simmer at a low heat for 15-20 more minutes. Serve hot and store in refrigerator. About 6-8 servings.

T'ibs We't is prepared on occasions as a main dish. It is very delicious with injera or bread and a little homemade yoghurt or cottage cheese.

GROUND BEEF STEW

ZIGNI WE'T

UTENSILS: medium cooking pot

INGREDIENTS:

1 lb.	ground beef (lean)
2 cups	red onions (chopped)
1/2 cup	red pepper (*berbere*) or red pepper paste (*awaze*)
2 cups	water
1 cup	butter (spiced)
1/4 tsp.	cardamom
1/4 tsp.	ginger
1/4 tsp.	bishop's weed
to taste	salt

PREPARATION: Fry *onions* without grease in a pan until they are brown. Add *red pepper* and *water* and stir. Add *butter*. Sprinkle *ground beef* into the pan while stirring. Add *spices* and let the stew cook until the meat is done. Serve hot. Store in refrigerator. Makes about 6-8 servings.

Zigni is somewhat similar to the Minchet Abish (spiced ground beef sauce) but a little milder and less spicy. It is also served as a main dish and can be served at any time with injera or bread.

GROUND BEEF STEW (MILD)

ZIGNI ALICH'A

UTENSILS: medium cooking pot

INGREDIENTS:
1 lb.	ground beef (lean)
2 cups	red onions (chopped)
2 cups	water
1 cup	butter (spiced)
1/4 tsp.	cardamom
1/4 tsp.	ginger (fresh)
1/4 tsp.	bishop's weed
1/4 tsp.	garlic (fresh)
to taste	salt

PREPARATION: Fry *onions* without grease in a pan, making sure onions don't change color. Add 1 cup of *water* and stir. Add *butter* and stir. Sprinkle *ground beef* into the pan while stirring. Add *cardamom, ginger, garlic, bishop's weed* and *salt*. Add a little *turmeric* for coloring and the remaining water and let the stew cook until the meat is done—20-30 minutes. Serve hot with injera or bread. Store in refrigerator. Makes about 6-8 servings.

Zigni Alich'a is somewhat similar to the Minchet Abish (spiced ground beef sauce) but milder and less spicy. It is also served as a main dish and can be served at any time.

GRILLED RIBS AND BEEF STEW

INSIRSIR

UTENSILS: medium cooking pot
medium frying pan

INGREDIENTS:

2 cups	red onions (chopped)
1/2 cup	red pepper (*berbere*) or red pepper paste (*awaze*)
1 cup	butter
6	ribs (beef or lamb)
1 lb.	meat with fat (beef or lamb)
1/3 cup	t'ej or wine
1/2 tsp.	black pepper
to taste	salt
1 cup	water

PREPARATION: Cook the *onions* in a pan until brown with a little water. Add *red pepper* and stir. Add *butter* and *ribs* and cook until meat is tender. Add *t'ej* or *wine* and stir. When stew is done add *salt* to taste and *black pepper*.

Take out the cooked ribs from the pot, and heat the frying pan without grease and fry the ribs for 10-15 minutes and set aside. Cut *meat with fat* into thin strips, sprinkle with the remaining *black pepper* and dip into stew. Serve meats hot separately or together side by side. Makes about 6 serving. Refrigerate to store.

Insirsir is an unusual dish, which may be served with a variety of vegetables, rice, noodles, injera or bread.

KIDNEY, LIVER IN SPICEY SAUCE

YEHODIQA WE'T

UTENSILS: 2 medium cooking pans
1 small cooking pan
1 medium frying pan

INGREDIENTS:

1 large	kidney (lamb or beef)
1/2	liver (lamb or beef)
2 cups	red onions (chopped)
1/4 cup	red pepper (*berbere*)
1/2 Tbsp.	ginger
1/2 cup	red cooking wine
1 cup	butter (spiced)
1/4 tsp.	false cardamom
1/4 tsp.	black pepper
2 cups	water
to taste	salt

PREPARATION: Cut *kidney, liver* separately into samll pieces. In a medium pan fry the kidney and liver on a low heat and set aside. Brown *onions* in a pan with *butter* and *cooking wine*. Add *red pepper* and stir. Add all the fried meat and stir. Add the 2 cups of water and simmer on very low heat till sauce thickens. Add *remaining spices* and cook 15-20 minutes. Serve hot. Store in refrigerator. Serves 6.

Yehodiqa We't is a delicacy.

KIDNEY, LIVER, INTESTINE & TRIPE COOKED IN SPICE

YEHODIQA T'IBS

UTENSILS: large frying pan

INGREDIENTS:

1/2 lb	kidney (lamb or beef)
1/2 lb	liver (lamb or beef)
1/2 lb	intestine (lamb or beef)
1/2 lb	tripe (lamb or beef)
1 cup	butter or oil (spiced)
1 1/2 cup	onion (chopped)
1/2 tsp	cardamon
1/4 tsp	garlic
1/4 tsp	black pepper
to taste salt	

PREPARATION: In running water, clean the tripe, liver, kidney & intestine thoroughly & cut separately in small sizes and set aside. In a large frying pan cook onions with butter or oil. Add the spices and mix well. Add the kidney, liver, intestine & tripe and cook for 5–8 minutes. When the mixture is done. Serve hot. Makes about 4–6 servings.

Yehodiqa T'ibs is prepared on special occasions. It is served with berbere or awaze & injera.

LEG OF LAMB IN HOT SAUCE

YEBEG INFILLE

UTENSILS: medium pot
medium pan
small mixing bowl

INGREDIENTS: 1   leg of lamb
1 cup   red onions (chopped)
1/2 cup   red pepper paste or
red pepper (*berbere*
or *awaze*)
1 cup   butter (spiced)
1/4 tsp.   ginger (fresh/minced)
1/4 tsp.   garlic (fresh/minced)
1/4 tsp.   black pepper,
to taste   salt
1 cup   t'ej or wine
1/4 tsp.   cardamom
2 cups   water

PREPARATION: Cut *meat* into thin strips leaving it attached to the bone. Boil the meat in enough water (not the two cups mentioned above) until it is tender or leave it raw and put aside. In a medium pan cook *onions* without grease until brown. In a little bowl, mix *butter* and *red pepper* and add to onion, stirring regularly. Add 2 cups *water* and simmer. Add *t'ej* and *spices*, and let sauces simmer on low heat for 20 minutes. When serving dip the boiled meat in hot sauce or serve sauce with injera. Yields 6-8 servings. Store in refrigerator.

MEAT COOKED IN SPICE
AND RED PEPPER

YESIGA T'IBS

UTENSILS: large frying pan

INGREDIENTS:

1 1/2 lbs.	beef (cut into cubes)
1/2 cup	butter (spiced)
1 1/2 cups	onions (chopped)
1 cup	red pepper (*berbere*)
1/2 tsp.	cardamom
1/4 tsp.	garlic (powder)
1/4 tsp.	black pepper
1/2 cup	t'ej or red wine
to taste	salt

PREPARATION: Cook *onions* without grease until they turn brownish red color. Add *butter, red pepper* (berbere) and stir. Add *wine* or *t'ej* stirring gently. In the same frying pan add the *beef* and cook for 5-10 minutes. Add *cardamom, garlic, black pepper* and *salt* to taste. When meat is done serve hot.

Yesiga t'ibs is prepared on all occasions. It is very delicious with injera or bread.

MILD BEEF STEW

YESIGA ALICH'A

UTENSILS: medium cooking pan or pot

INGREDIENTS:

3 cups	water
2 cups	red onions (chopped)
2 lbs.	beef with bones
2 cups	butter
1/2 tsp.	ginger
1/4 tsp.	garlic
2 fresh	green pepper (chili Anaheim)
to taste	salt
1/4 tsp.	turmeric

PREPARATION: At a medium heat, *cook onions lightly* without grease in a deep frying pan. (Make sure it does not burn.) Before the onion starts to turn brown add 2 cups of *water*. Stirring occasionally add the *beef with bones* after it has been cut into small pieces and let it cook for 20 minutes. Add *butter* and *garlic* and stir. Add *ginger* and *salt* and let it simmer. (A touch of *turmeric* will give it a nice color.) Seed and slice *green peppers* and add to the sauce with the remaining 1 cup water. Cook for about 10 more minutes. Remove from heat and serve hot. Cover and store in refrigerator. Serves about 6-8.

Yesiga Alich'a is a milder version of Yesiga we't. It is delicious and colorful main dish. Eaten with injera or bread.

MILD BEEF STEW WITH RIBS

SIKSIKOSH

UTENSILS: large cooking pot or pan

INGREDIENTS:
6 medium	ribs
1 lb.	ground beef
1/2 cup	red pepper (*berbere*)
2 cups	red onions (chopped)
1 cup	butter (spiced)
1/2 cup	t'ej or wine
1 cup	water
to taste	salt

PREPARATION: Cook *onions* without grease in a pan until they are gold. Add *water* and stir well. Add the *ribs, butter*, and *red pepper* and cook until the *meat* is tender. Add *t'ej* or *wine* a little at a time and stir. Add the *ground beef* and cook until it is well done. Simmer for about 10 minutes on a low heat, add the spices and remove from the heat. Serve immediately. Makes 6 servings. Store in refrigerator in a covered container.

Siksikosh is a dish prepared mainly with leftover meat. It is mild and nourishing and not too complicated to cook. Eat with injera or bread.

116

MILD FRIED BEEF STEW

T'IBS ALICH'A

UTENSILS: medium frying pan
medium cooking pot

INGREDIENTS:
2 cups	red onions (chopped)
2 cups	butter (spiced)
2 lbs.	meat (beef cut in cubes)
1/2 tsp.	garlic
1 tsp.	ginger
1/4 tsp.	black pepper
1/4 tsp.	turmeric
2-3 fresh	green pepper (optional)
2 cups	water
to taste	salt

PREPARATION: Cook *onions* over a low heat without grease making sure it does not burn. (Burning changes the color of the sauce.) Add *butter* and stir.

In a separate pan, fry the *meat*, without grease, until it is tender. Add the meat to the *onions* and stir gently. Add *spices* while still stirring and cook for 15-20 minutes. Add the *water*, stir and let it simmer. Wash and cut *green peppers* into long slices and gently dip into the sauce. Serve hot and refrigerate to store. About 6-8 servings.

T'ibs Alich'a, like the we't, is prepared on occasion. It makes a nice main dish. It is very delicious with injera or bread.

MILD SAUSAGE STEW

YEQWALIMA ALICH'A

UTENSILS: medium cooking pan
medium mixing bowl
needle and threads

INGREDIENTS:

1 cup	red onions (minced)
2 cups	butter (spiced)
1/4 cup	garlic
1/4 tsp.	ginger
1/4 tsp.	black pepper
to taste	salt
3 1/2 cups	water

PREPARATION: Brown *onions* without grease in a pan making
sure they don't burn by adding a little water at
a time. Add 1 cup *butter*, 1/4 tsp. *ginger*, 1/4
tsp. *black pepper*, 1/4 cup *garlic* and set aside.

In the mixing bowl put the ground beef and
add the following ingredients except the intestine. Blend well.

1 lb.	ground beef
1 cup	butter (spiced)
1/4 Tbsp.	garlic powder
1/4 tsp.	ginger
1/4 tsp.	black pepper
to taste	salt

1/2 lb.	intestine (lamb)

Clean intestine in running water thoroughly.
Stuff the mixture into the *intestine*. Tie and cut
into small sausages. Add the sausages to the

cooked onions one at a time and stir. Add the rest of the cups of water and cook until stew is thick for 20-30 minutes. Serve hot. Makes about 6 servings. Store in refrigerator.

Yeqwalima Alich'a is a mild version of the We't without the red pepper.

Sausages

MINCED MEAT STEW SLIGHTLY DRY

DEREQ WE'T

UTENSILS: 2 medium cooking pots

INGREDIENTS:

2 cups	red onions (chopped)
2 lb.	ribs
2 lb.	minced meat
2 cup	butter (spiced)
1/2 cup	red pepper (*berbere*)
1/4 tsp.	garlic powder
1/2 tsp.	ginger powder
to taste	salt
2 cups	wine or t'ej

PREPARATION: Cook the *onion* till it changes its color. Add the *berbere*, *butter* and stir gently. Set aside. Add *ribs* and cook together. After adding the ribs add *wine* or *t'ej* add the spices and stir gently. Add *minced meat* and keep stirring and cook for 15 minutes. Be sure that it will not be over cooked.

Dereq We't is similar to Minchet Abish.

RAW BEEF IN SPICEY SAUCE

LEMLEM ZIGIN

UTENSILS: medium cooking pan

INGREDIENTS:

2 cups	red onions (chopped)
1 tsp.	red pepper (*berbere*)
2 cups	water
1 cup	butter (*spiced*)
1/4 cup	garlic
1/3 cup	cooking wine (red) or t'ej
2 lbs.	meat with bones
1/4 tsp.	black pepper
1/2 tsp.	ginger
1/4 tsp.	cardamom
2 lbs.	ground beef
to taste	salt

PREPARATION: Brown *onions* without grease in medium cooking pan. Add *meat with bones* and cook until tender. Add *red pepper* and a little *wine* or *t'ej* at a time and stir constantly. Add *butter* and stir. Add *spices* and *water* and simmer for 10-20 minutes more. When sauce is thick put ground beef in a dish and pour the sauce on it. Serves 6. Store meat and sauce separately in refrigerator.

Lemlem Zigin is a delicious meal for people who like their meat rare and at the same time favor the spicy sauce.

RAW MEAT

T'IRE SIGA

UTENSILS: medium serving plate
small serving bowl

INGREDIENTS: 2 lb.   red beef (botom round)
3-4 tsp.   red pepper (*berbere*), red pepper
paste (*awaze*) mit'mit'a (hot
red pepper) (serrano)
1/2 cup   t'ej or wine

PREPARATION: Cut *meat into big chunks or cubes. Mix red
pepper* (berbere) in *t'ej* or *wine* in a small serving bowl. If *afring* and *mit'mit'a*, serve powdered. Serve meat at room temperature with
injera or crisp bread. Makes 4 servings. Refrigerate to store.

T'ire Siga is a popular Ethiopian dish, especially among men. It
is a tasty, east to serve, all occasion dish, and is the main attraction at any meal.

SHREDDED BEEF STEW

SALAYISH

UTENSILS: cooking pot (medium)
a pan
covered container
small bowl

INGREDIENTS:

2 cups	red onions (chopped)
1 tsp.	garlic
1/2 cup	red pepper (*berbere*)
to taste	salt
1/2 cup	butter (spiced)
1/2 tsp.	ginger
1/2 tsp.	false cardamom
1 lb.	meat with bone
4 cups	water
1/4 tsp.	black pepper

PREPARATION: Fry *onions* without grease in a pan over a low heat and stir. *Do not brown*. Cut *meat* in long strips and add to the onions. Add *water* and stir. Add the *spices*. In a little bowl mix *butter* and *red pepper* and then add to the stew. When the stew thickens add salt and *black pepper* and remove from heat. Serves 6-8. Store in refrigerator in covered container.

Salayish is beef strips simmered in red pepper sauce. It is best eaten with injera as a main dish. Serve hot for a light lunch.

SLIGHTLY COOKED BEEF TARTAR

KITFO LEB LEB

UTENSILS: medium cooking pan

INGREDIENTS:

2 lbs.	red meat only (beef)
1 cup	butter (spiced)
1 Tbsp.	hot red pepper (*mit'mit'a*) (serrano)
1 Tbsp.	false cardamom
1/4 tsp.	black pepper
1/4 cup	red onions (chopped)-optional
to taste	salt

PREPARATION: Chop or grind *beef* into (preferably by hand) small pieces like ground beef. In a medium cooking pan, melt *butter* for 5 minutes. Add *spices* and remove from heat. Add ground beef and mit'mit'a and mix well. Cook Kitfo lightly rare over a low heat making sure it is not overcooked. Serve hot with a side order of cottage cheese preferably home made. Makes about 4 servings. Store in refrigerator.

Kitfo Leb Leb is just a variation of Kitfo for those who prefer their meat cooked. It tastes delicious.

SPICED GROUND BEEF STEW (HOT)

MINCHET ABISH

UTENSILS: medium cooking pan
medium mixing bowl

INGREDIENTS:

2 lbs.	ground beef
2 cups	red onions (chopped)
1 cup	red pepper (*berbere*)
2 cups	water
2 cups	butter (spiced)
to taste	salt
1/4 tsp.	ginger
1/4 tsp.	shiro (pea flour)
1/4 tsp.	cardamom
1/4 tsp.	cloves
1 cup	red cooking wine or t'ej
1/4 tsp.	fenugreek

PREPARATION: Brown *onions* in medium pan with *fenugreek*. Add *meat* and stir until all the juice from the meat evaporates. Add *butter* and *salt* and cook for 15 minutes and then add *ginger* and *wine* or *t'ej* in the mixing bowl, make a thick paste with *shiro* and *water* and add the paste to thicken the sauce. Sprinkle *cardamom* and mix well. Add *cloves*. When meat is soft and tender remove from the heat and serve hot. Warm leftover stew on low heat. Serves about 6. Refrigerate to store.

Minchet Abish is a very delicious stew. Eat it hot with injera or bread.

SPICED GROUND BEEF STEW (MILD)

MINCHET ABISH ALICH'A

UTENSILS: medium cooking pan
small bowl for mixing

INGREDIENTS:

2 lbs.	ground beef
2 cups	red onions (chopped)
1/4 tsp.	fenugreek
2 cups	butter (spiced)
to taste	salt
1/2 ts.	ginger
1/4 tsp	shiro (pea flour)
2 cups	water
1/2 cup	white cooking wine (optional)
1/4 tsp.	turmeric
1/2 tsp.	garlic fresh (minced)

PREPARATION: Cook *onions* in pan with *fenugreek* making sure not to burn. Add *meat* and stir until the juice evaporates. Add *butter* and *salt* and cook for 15 minutes and then add *ginger* and *wine*. In a little bowl make a thick paste of *shiro* and *water* and add to thicken the sauce. Sprinkle *turmeric* for coloring and mix well. Add *garlic*. When meat is soft and tender remove from heat and serve hot. Warm left over stew on low heat. Serves about 6. Refrigerate to store.

Minchet Abish Alich'a is just a milder version of Minchet Abish stew. It is a delicious and colorful main dish, eaten with injera or bread.

126

SPICED SAUSAGE STEW

YEQWALIMA WE'T

UTENSILS: medium cooking pan
medium mixing bowl
needle and threads

INGREDIENTS: 1 cup   red onions (minced)
1 cup   butter (spiced)
1/2 cup   red pepper (*berbere*)
1/4 tsp.   garlic
1/4 tsp.   false cardamom
1/4 tsp.   ginger
1/4 tsp.   black pepper
3 1/2 cups   water
to taste   salt

PREPARATION: Brown *onions* without grease in a pan *making sure they don't burn* by adding a little water at a time. Add 1 cup *butter* and 1/2 cup *red pepper*. Stir for 10 minutes. Add 2 1/2 cups of *water*. Add all the remaining ingredients. Stir for 10 more minutes and set aside.

In the mixing bowl put the ground beef and add the following ingredients except the intestine. Blend well.

1 lb.   ground beef
1 cup   butter (spiced)
1/4 tsp.   garlic powder
1/4 tsp.   false cardamom
1/4 tsp.   ginger
1/4 tsp.   black pepper
to taste   salt

1/2 lb.   intestine (lamb)

127

Clean intestine in running water thoroughly. Stuff the mixture into the *intestine* and tie into small sausages. Cut. Add the sausages to the cooked onions one at a time and stir. Add the rest of the cups of water and cook until the stew is thick, for 25-30 minutes. Serve hot. Makes about 6 servings. Store in refrigerator.

Yeqwalima We't is made on special occasions due to the long preparation period. But it is a tasty dish which can be served with injera or bread.

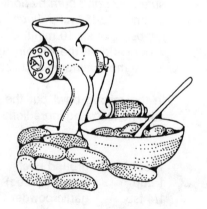

Sausages

STEAK TARTAR

KITFO

UTENSILS: medium pan
medium bowl

INGREDIENTS:

2 lbs.	red meat only (beef)
1 cup	buter (spiced)
1 Tbsp.	hot red pepper (*mit'mit'a*) (serrano)
1 Tbsp.	false cardamom
1/4 tsp.	black pepper
to taste	salt

PREPARATION: Chop or grind *beef* into (preferably by hand) small pieces like ground beef. In a medium cooking pan, melt butter in low heat. Add *spices* and remove from heat. Add ground beef and *mit'mit'a* and mix well. Serve hot. Makes about 4 servings. Store in refrigerator.

Kitfo is the most popular Ethiopian dish. With injera or bread and a side order of homemade cottage cheese and spiced collard greens, there is nothing like it.

SPICED TRIPE, LIVER AND BEEF

DULLET

UTENSILS: medium cooking pan

INGREDIENTS:

1 lb.	tripe (lamb)
1 lb.	liver (lamb)
1 lb.	minced beef (lean)
1 Tbsp.	red pepper (*berbere*)
3 medium	green pepper chopped (chili Anaheim)
1/3 cup	red onions (chopped)
1 cup	buter (spiced)
1/4 tsp.	black pepper
1/4 tsp.	cardamom
to taste	salt

PREPARATION: In running water, clean the *tripe* and *liver*. Separately mince tripe, liver and *beef* and set aside. In a medium pan cook *onions* with butter and turn off the heat. Add the *spices* and mix well. Add all the meat and mix gently. Serves 4-6. Store in refrigerator.

Dullet is another popular dish which may be served for brunch, lunch or dinner. Best eaten with injera and a side order of cottage cheese.

SPICED BEEF STEW

YESIGA WE'T

UTENSILS: medium pan—4-6 quarts
covered container

INGREDIENTS:

2 cups	chopped onions
3 cups	water
1/2 cup	red pepper (*berbere*)
2 cups	butter (spiced)
2 lbs.	beef with bone (or lamb)
1/2 tsp.	ginger
1/4 tsp.	garlic
1 tsp.	red cooking wine or t'ej
to taste	salt

PREPARATION: Brown *onions* without grease in a frying pan at medium heat. Chop the *beef* and *bone* into small pieces and add them to the cooking onions. Add *red pepper*, stirring occasionally, until the meat is tender. Add the *butter* and cooking *wine* or *t'ej* and stir. Add *water* and stir until we't is thick. Add *garlic, ginger,* and *salt* to taste. Let sauce simmer for a while until the meat is tender enough to pierce easily with the point of a sharp knife. Remove from heat and serve hot. To store put in covered container and refrigerate. Serves 6.

Yesiga We't is a main dish. It may be eaten for lunch or dinner with either injera or bread.

STUFFED TRIPE STEW

ISKUNFUR

UTENSILS: medium cooking pot or pan
medium mixing bowl
needle and thread

INGREDIENTS:

1 lb.	tripe (beef or lamb)
2 cups	red onions (chopped)
1/2 cup	red pepper (*berbere*)
1/4 Tbsp.	false cardamom
1/4 tsp.	ginger
1/4 tsp.	garlic
1/4 tsp.	black pepper
2 cups	water
1 cup	butter (spiced)

PREPARATION: Cook *onions* without grease in a pan. Mix *red pepper* and *butter* in a bowl and add to the onions. Set aside. Scrape and wash *tripe* under running water and cut into 4-inch to 6-inch squares.

Stuffing: Mix the following ingredients: put about a tablespoonful of the mixture in the tripe squares and sew them up with needle and thread.

INGREDIENTS:

1 Tbsp.	butter (spiced)
1 Tbsp.	red onions (chopped)
1/4 Tbsp.	false cardamom
1/4 Tbsp.	ginger
1/4 Tbsp.	black pepper
to taste	salt
1 cup	cooked rice (optional)

PREPARATION: Put the stuffed tripes into the pan of cooked onions and add enough of the 2 cups of water to cover them. Cook until the sauce thickens and add the rest of the water. Simmer for about 10-15 minutes and remove from the heat. Serve hot. Makes 6 servings. Store in refrigerator in a covered container.

Iskunfur is a delicious sauce prepared for special occasions. It may be eaten with injera or bread as a main dish or served with rice and vegetables as a side dish.

TRIPE AND TONGUE COOKED IN FENUGREEK

HULBET MEREKH

UTENSILS: 6-8 quart pot
10-12 inch pan

INGREDIENTS:

2 lbs.	tripe (beef or lamb)
2 lbs.	tongue (beef or lamb)
1 Tbsp.	fenugreek
2 Tbsp.	red pepper (*berbere*)
2 cups	finely chopped onions
1 Tbsp.	finely coppped garlic or garlic powder
1 cup	butter (spiced)
to taste	salt
2 tsps.	ground cardamom
2 tsps.	coriander

PREPARATION: Place the *tripe* and the *tongue* in a heavy 6 to 8 quart pot. Pour water to cover the tripe and tongue by at least 2 inches. Bring to boil over high heat. Reduce heat to low and simmer partially covered for 1 1/2 to 2 hours or until the tripe is tender and shows no resistance when pierced with the sharp point of a knife. Drain the tripe and the tongue and rinse in cold water. Put the tongue aside and rinse the tripe in cold running water. Discard any globules of fat from the inner side of the tripe. Cut the tripe and tongue about 1 inch wide and 2 inches long.

Cook *onions* in a heavy 10 to 12 inch pan over moderate heat for 5 to 6 minutes, until they are soft and brown. Add the *butter* and stir. When the butter sputters add the *spices* and keep stirring over low heat for 5 minutes. Add the tripe and the tongue with 4 to 6 cups of water. Cover the pan and simmer for 1 1/2 to 2 hours. Serving 6 to 8.

Hulbet merekh is served over a layer of injera and also with boiled rice.

TONGUE COOKED IN SPICE

YEMILAS T'IBS

UTENSILS: frying pan
large cooking pan

INGREDIENTS:

1 lb	tongue
1 cup	onions (chopped)
1/2 cup	butter (spiced)
1/4 tsp	cardamon
1/4 tsp	black pepper
1/2 Tbsp	garlic (mashed)
1/4 tsp	ginger
6 cups	water

PREPARATION: Wash and scrap tongue and boil in 6 cups of water. When tender, remove the tongue and peel. Slice the tongue into 1/2 inch thin. Set aside.
In a frying pan cook onions. Add butter and the spices—and mix well. Add the tongue one by one and cook for 6–10 minutes. When tongue is cooked add salt to taste. Serve hot. Makes about 4–5 servings.

Yemilas T'ibs is another variety of cooked meat prepared only on special occasions. It is served with awaze and injera.

136

TONGUE AND TRIPE

MILASINA SEMBER

UTENSILS: large cooking pot
medium frying pan

INGREDIENTS:

2 cups	red onions (chopped0
1 lb.	tongue (beef)
1 medium	tripe (beef or lamb)
1/2 cup	butter (spiced)
1/2 Tbsp.	ginger (fresh mashed)
1/4 Tbsp.	garlic (fresh mashed)
1/4 tsp.	black pepper
to taste	salt
1 small can	tomato paste
6 cups	water

PREPARATION: Wash and scrape *tongue* and *tripe* and boil in 6 cups of *water*. Keep the water. When tender, remove the tripe and tongue and peel tongue. Cut tripe and tongue into 1 or 2 inch cubes and set aside. In a medium pan brown *onions* lightly. Add *tomato paste* and *butter* and mix well. Add 2 cups boiling water used for cooking tongue and tripe. Stir gently. Add tripe and tongue. When sauce thickens add 3 cups water. Add *spices* and blend well. Simmer for 10-15 minutes and serve hot. Serves 6. Store in refrigerator.

Milasina sember is a rich, delicious dish served with injera or bread. Carrots may be added to it for variety.

BLUE NILE RESTAURANT'S INTERIOR SET UP

GURSHA/FEEDING A GUEST BY PLACING CHUNKS OF FOOD INTO HIS OR HER MOUTH.

Photo compliments of **Kestedamena Restaurant**
5779 W. Venice Blvd., Los Angeles, Calif   (213) 933-6522

MESOB/TRADITIONAL FOOD SETTING.

Photo compliments of **Wanza Ethiopian Cuisine**
6409 Roosvelt Way NE, Seattle, Washington   (206) 525-3950
Copyright © 1989, Barry Gregg

Photo compliments of **C & K Importing**, 2791 W. Pico Blvd., Los Angeles, Calif. (213) 737-2970 — for description of spices see page 255

GINFILFIL/INJERA IN SAUCE MIXED OVER LOW FIRE p. 205

*Photo compliments of **Blue Nile Restaurant***
2525 Telegraph Ave., Berkeley, Calif   (415) 540-6777

BARLEY OR WHEAT PORRIDGE/GENFO p. 217

*Photo compliments of **Kokeb Restaurant***
926 12th Ave., Seattle, Washington   (206) 322-0485

ASSORTED SNACKS p. 23-45

*Photo Compliments of **Tsige Moya**, 7409 Caroll Lane, Falls Church, VA. (703) 573-8602*

BREAD/ASSORTED
ETHIOPIAN BREAD p. 85-100

ASSORTED DISHES

*Photo Compliments of **Meskerem Restaurant**, 2434 18th St. NW, Washington, D.C. (202) 462-4100*

COFFEE/TRADITIONAL ETHIOPIAN SETTING p. 66

*Photo Compliments of **Meskerem Restaurant**, 2434 18th St. NW, Washington, D.C. (202) 462-4100*

INJERA-"AENJERA" MOSES' MANNA, ABRAHAM'S BREAD/TRADITIONAL ETHIOPIAN BREAD p. 79

*Photo Compliments of **Aenjera Bakery,** 4554 Eisenhower Avenue, Alex., VA, 22304. (703) 823-9356*

DULLET/SPICED TRIPE, LIVER AND BEEF p. 130

*Photo Compliments of **Fasika's Ethiopian Cuisine,** 2447 18th St. NW, Washington, D.C. (202) 797-7673*

MESKEREM RESTAURANT'S INTERIOR SET UP

*Photo Compliments of **Meskerem Restaurant,** 2434 18th St. NW, Washington, D.C. (202) 462-4100*

COMBINATION/FOOD SERVED IN A WIDE PLATTER

*Photo Compliments of **Fasika's Ethiopian Cuisine**, 2447 18th St. NW, Washington, D.C. (202) 797-7673*

LEGUMES AND VEGETABLE DISHES p. 183–200

*Photo Compliments of **Rosalinds Restaurant**, 1044 S Fairfax Ave L.A. Calif (213) 936-2486.*

GOMEN/COLLARD GREENS p. 166

TEEMATEEM FITFIT/TOMATOES BLENDED IN SPICES AND INJERA p. 204

*Photo Compliments of **Blue Nile Restaurant,** 103 W. 77th St. at Columbus Ave., N.Y. City (212) 580-3232*

*Photo Compliments of **Sheba Restaurant,** 3109 Telegraph Ave., Oakland, CA (415) 654-3741*

YEATAKILT ALICH'A/VEGETABLE STEW p. 180

*Photo Compliments of **Red Sea Ethiopian Cuisine,** 2463 18th St., Washington, D.C. (202) 483-5000*

DORO W'ET/HOT CHICKEN STEW p. 142

*Photo Compliments of **Red Sea Ethiopian Cuisine,** 2463 18th St. NW, Washington, D.C. (202) 483-5000*

DORO ALICH'A/MILD CHICKEN STEW p. 147

*Photo Compliments of **Blue Nile Restaurant,** 317 Braun ct, Ann Arbor, MI (313) 663-3116*

YESIGA W'ET/HOT SPICED BEEF STEW p. 131

*Photo Compliments of **Queen Of Sheba,** 5778 Rodeo Road, Los Angeles, CA (213) 296-1070*

YESIGA ALICH'A/MILD BEEF STEW p. 115

*Photo Compliments of **Nyala Restaurant,** 39 Grove St. San Francisco, CA (415) 861-0788*

MESOB/TRADITIONAL ETHIOPIAN SETTING

*Photo Compliments of **Blue Nile Restaurant,** 103 W. 77th St. at Columbus Ave., N.Y. City* · *(212) 580-3232*

YESHIMBRA FITFIT/WHOLE DRIED CHICK PEA SAUCE BLENDED IN SPICES AND INJERA p. 212

Photo Compliments of **Red Sea Ethiopian Cuisine,** *2463 18th St. NW, Washington, D.C. (202) 483-5000*

ASSA W'ET/HOT FISH STEW p. 156, 158

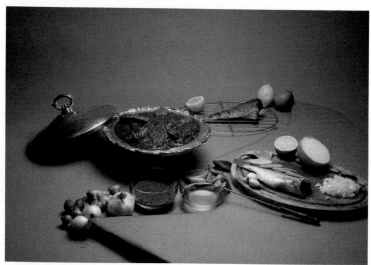

Photo Compliments of **Blue Nile Restaurant,** *103 W. 77th St. at Columbus Ave., N.Y. City (212) 580-3232*

LEGUMES AND VEGETABLE DISHES p. 183–200

Photo Compliments of **Rasselas Restaurant,** 2801 California St., San Francisco, CA (415) 567-5010
for description of dishes see page 255

ASSORTED DISHES

Photo Compliments of **Meskerem Restaurant,** 2434 18th St. NW, Washington, D.C. (202) 462-4100
for description of dishes see page 255

Chicken Dishes

The secret of a good *we't* is to fry the onions until they are limp and can be mashed with a spoon for easy blending in with the *berbere* and butter mixture, after which the different ingredients form a smooth consistency. When the different constituents separate it is a bad *we't*.

Constant stirring is also absolutely necessary, especially during the initial stage of cooking. Otherwise the onion and *berbere* will stick to the bottom of the cooking utensil and burn giving a bad aroma to the *we't*.

CHICKEN DIPPED IN HOT SAUCE

YEDORO INFILLE

UTENSILS: large bowl
medium cooking pan
medium cooking pot

INGREDIENTS:

1 whole	chicken
1 cup	red onions (chopped)
1/4 cup	red pepper (*berbere*)
1 cup	butter (spiced)
2 cups	water
to taste	salt
1/4 tsp.	black pepper
1 Tbsp.	ginger
1 Tbsp.	garlic

PREPARATION: Skin *chicken* and cut into usual pieces. Put aside smaller pieces (neck, wings, etc.). Leave the meat attached to the bones and cut chicken into strips and put aside. In a medium pan, brown *onions* with one cup *butter* and add *red pepper* and stir gently. Add one cup of *water* at a time and stir well. Take large chicken pieces and add to cooked onions. Add *salt* and the rest of *ginger, garlic* and *black pepper.* Cook for 20-30 minutes adding the remaining water. In another pan boil the rest of the small pieces of chicken with some onion for 15 minutes. Remove the smaller chicken parts from the water and dip into prepared sauce. Serve hot. Good for about 6 servings. Store in refrigerator.

Yedoro Infille is best eaten with injera, and the sauce mixed with some yoghurt or served by itself as a main dish.

CHICKEN STEW

DORO WE'T

UTENSILS: large bowl
medium cooking pot or pan

INGREDIENTS:

1 whole	chicken
6 cups	red onions (chopped)
1 cup	red pepper (*berbere*)
2 cups	butter (spiced)
1/4 tsp.	false cardamom
1/4 tsp.	black pepper
1/4 tsp.	bishop's weed
1/4 tsp.	garlic powder
1/2 tsp.	ginger
to taste	salt
1/2 cup	t'ej or red wine
4 cups	water
6 medium	eggs (hard boiled)
1 medium	lime

PREPARATION: Remove skin from *chicken*, cut into the usual parts, and wash several times in water. Wash and cut *lime* into 4 pieces, add to a large bowl of clean water and soak chicken in it. In a medium pan cook *onions* until golden brown. Add *butter*. Add *red pepper* and mix well. Add about 1/2 cup of *water* and stir. Add *t'ej* or *wine*. Add the *spices* and blend well. Add prepared chicken pieces and cook for about 30-40 minutes. Add more water and stir gently so as not to separate the meat from the bones. Add salt and stir. When sauce begins to thicken, sprinkle with *black pepper*. Add *hard-boiled eggs* to the sauce and serve hot. Makes 6 servings. Store in refrigerator.

Doro We't is a most popular Ethiopian dish served on special occasions with injera and a side order of yoghurt or homemade cottage cheese. May be eaten with bread or rice.

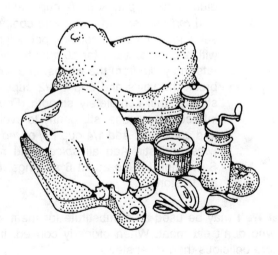

Whole chicken

EGG SAUCE

YENQULAL WE'T

UTENSILS: medium cooking pot
small cooking pot
small mixing bowl

INGREDIENTS:

1 cup	onions (chopped)
1/4 cup	red pepper (*berbere*)
1 cup	butter (spiced)
1/4 cup	t'ej or red cooking wine
6	egg yolks
1 tsp.	ginger (freshly minced)
1/4 tsp.	black pepper
to taste	salt
4 cups	water

PREPARATION: Cook *red onions* brown without grease in medium cooking pot. Add 1/2 cup *water* and stir. Add *red pepper* and *butter* and cook well and set aside. In a small cooking pot boil the *eggs* with 2 cups of water for 10 minutes and separate the *yolks* from the whites. In a small bowl break the yolks and add 1 1/2 cups of water stirring until completely smooth. Pour slowly into cooking sauce, stir gently to avoid lumps and cook well. Add 1/4 cup *t'ej* or *red cooking wine* and stir. Add all *spices* and mix well. Serve hot. Makes about 6 servings. Refrigerate to store.

Yenqulal We't may be used as a substitute for meat stews for people who don't eat meat. When properly cooked, it can be much more delicious than meat stews.

FRIED CHICKEN

YEDORO T'IBS

UTENSILS: deep large frying pan
large bowl

INGREDIENTS: 1 medium   chicken
1 cup   butter or oil
1 cup   red onions (chopped)
1/4 tsp.   black pepper
1/2 cup   wine
to taste   salt
6 cups   water

PREPARATION: Skin and wash *chicken* and cut into usual
parts. Boil in 6 cups of *water* until tender. In a
separate pan, fry chopped *onions* with *butter*
until golden brown. Add a little *wine* at a time.
Add boiled chicken and cook. Sprinkle *black
pepper* and *salt* and serve hot. Serves 6. Refrigerate to store.

Yedoro T'ibs may be cooked with a little red pepper if desired.

HOT MINCED CHICKEN STEW (HOT)

YEDORO MINCHET ABISH

UTENSILS: medium cooking pan
large bowl

INGREDIENTS:

1 medium	chicken (whole)
2 cups	red onions (chopped)
1/2 cup	red pepper (*berbere*)
2 cups	water
2 cups	butter (spiced)
1/4 tsp.	garlic (minced)
1/4 tsp.	ginger (minced)
1/4 tsp.	black pepper
1/4 tsp.	cardamom
1/2 cup	t'ej or wine
to taste	salt

PREPARATION: Skin *chicken*, wash good, debone and mince the meat only. Brown *onions* in medium pan until cooked well and soft. Add *butter, red pepper* and *salt* and cook for 20 minutes and then add *ginger* and *wine*. Add minced chicken meat and cook gently for 10 minutes. Add *water* and the *spices* and cook stirring gently for another 15 minutes or until the water evaporates and stew is thick. Makes 6 servings. Store in refrigerator.

Yedoro Minchet Abish is a very versatile hot stew. Eat it hot with injera or bread. Serve it as a sauce for rice or pasta. Make sandwiches for a snack or appetizer. Good for breakfast, lunch and dinner, and for special occasions.

MILD CHICKEN STEW

DORO ALICH'A

UTENSILS: large bowl
medium cooking pot

INGREDIENTS:

1 whole	chicken
6 cups	red onions (chopped)
2 cups	butter (spiced)
1/4 tsp.	black pepper
1/4 tsp.	bishop's weed
1/4 tsp.	garlic powder
1/4 tsp.	ginger
1/2 cup	t'ej or white wine
to taste	salt
4 cups	water
6 medium	eggs (hard boiled)
1 medium	lime

PREPARATION: Remove skin from the *chicken*, cut into the usual parts, and wash several times in *water*. Wash and cut lime into 4 pieces, add to a large bowl of clean water and soak chicken in it. In a medium pan *cook onions, making sure they don't burn*. Add *butter* and mix well. Add about 1/2 cup of water and stir. Add *t'ej* or *wine*. Add the *spices* and blend well. Add prepared chicken pieces and cook for about 45 minutes. Add more water and stir gently so as not to separate the meat from the bones. Add *salt* and stir. When sauce begins to thicken, sprinkle with *black pepper*. Add *hard boiled* eggs to the sauce. Serve hot. Makes 6 servings. Store in refrigerator.

Doro Alich'a is just like Doro We't without the red pepper. It is a very delicious dish as well.

147

MILD MINCED CHICKEN STEW (MILD)

YEDORO MINCHET ABISH (ALICH'A)

UTENSILS: medium cooking pan
large bowl

INGREDIENTS:

1 medium	chicken (whole)
2 cups	red onions (chopped)
2 cups	water
1 cup	butter (spiced)
1/4 tsp.	garlic (minced)
1/4 tsp.	ginger (minced)
1/4 tsp.	black pepper
1/4 tsp.	cardamom
1/2 cup	white wine or t'ej
to taste	salt

PREPARATION: Skin *chicken*, wash good, debone and mince the meat only. Cook *onions* in medium pan, making sure they don't burn. Add *butter, salt*, and cook for 20 minutes and then add *ginger* and *wine*. Add minced chicken meat and cook gently for 10 minutes. Add water and the *spices* cook stirring gently for another 15 minutes or until the water evaporates and stew is thick. Makes 6 servings. Store in refrigerator.

Yedoro Minchet Abish Alich'a is a very versatile mild stew. Eat it hot with injera or bread.

Fish Dishes

Different *we'ts* are prepared for fasting and non-fasting days. If prepared from ingredients of animal origin such as beef, poultry or eggs, then it is a non-fasting food.

CURRIED FISH STEW

YE'ASSA ALICH'A

UTENSILS: medium cooking pan
medium frying pan

INGREDIENTS:

3 medium	fish fillets
2 cups	red onions (chopped)
1 cup	oil
1 1/2 cups	water
1/4 tsp.	black pepper
1/2 cup	white wine or *t'ej*
to taste	salt
1/4 tsp.	turmeric

PREPARATION: Cut *fish fillets* in small pieces and grill lightly without grease and set aside. In a separate pan, cook *red onions* until lightly brown. Add *wine* or *t'ej* a little at a time and add *turmeric*. Add *oil* and cook sauce for 15 minutes making sure it does not burn by adding water a little at a time. When sauce is ready add the grilled fish, *black pepper* and *salt* to taste. Simmer for 5-10 minutes on low heat and serve hot. 4-6 servings, refrigerate to store.

Ye'assa Alich'a is a milder version of Ye'assa We't without red pepper. This replaces beef curry when fasting.

DRIED FISH STEW

YE'ASSA ZILBO

UTENSILS: medium cooking pan

INGREDIENTS:

2 lbs.	dried fish cut in strips
2 cups	red onions (chopped)
1/2 tsp.	fenugreek
1/4 tsp.	red pepper (*berbere*)
1 cup	oil
1 tsp.	garlic
1/2 tsp.	ginger
1/4 tsp.	cardamom
to taste	black pepper
1/4 tsp.	salt
1/3 cup	*t'ej* or wine
2 cups	water

PREPARATION: Brown *onions* with *fenugreek* adding a little *water* at a time to keep from burning and stir. Add *red pepper* and *oil* and mix well. Add *t'ej*. Add *fish* to the cooking pot. Add water, stirring gently until the dried fish softens. Add *spices* and blend well. Serve hot. Yields 4-6 servings. Refrigerate to store.

Ye'assa Zilbo is a slight variety of Ye'assa W'et. It is also served with injera or bread during periods of fasting or as a vegetarian dish.

FISH DIPPED IN HOT SAUCE

YE'ASSA INFILLE

UTENSILS: medium cooking pan medium frying pan

INGREDIENTS:
4 medium	fish fillets
2 cups	red onions (chopped)
1 cup	split peas
3 cups	water
1/2 cup	red pepper (*berbere*) or red pepper paste (*awaze*)
1 cup	oil
1/2 cup	wine or *t'ej*
1/4 tsp.	black pepper
to taste	salt

PREPARATION: Boil *split peas* in 3 cups of *water* for 15 minutes and add *red onions*. Add *red pepper* and *oil* and stir gently. Add *t'ej* or *wine* and cook for 10-15 minutes. Sprinkle *black pepper* and *salt*. Cut *fish* into thin strips and dip in hot cooking sauce for about 5 minutes before serving. Serve hot. Refrigerate to store. Makes 4-6 servings.

Ye'assa Infille makes a nice meal with injera or bread or may be served on toothpicks as appetizers.

FISH TARTAR

YE'ASSA KITFO

UTENSILS: medium mixing bowl

INGREDIENTS:

4 medium	fresh fish fillets
1/4 cup	red pepper (*berbere*)
1/2 cup	oil
1/2 cup	*t'ej* or wine
1/4 tsp.	black pepper
2	chopped green pepper (chili Anaheim or Jalapeño)
to taste	salt
1	lemon

PREPARATION: Cut *fish* into small pieces. Mix *red pepper* or *red pepper paste, oil, wine* or *t'ej, salt, black pepper*. Chop *green pepper*, add to fish and red pepper mixture. Add *lemon juice* and serve cold. Cover and refrigerate to store. Makes 4 to 6 servings.

Ye'assa Kitfo is raw fish harmoniously blended with spices and red pepper.

Fish

FISH WITH COLLARD GREENS

ASSA BEGOMEN

UTENSILS: medium cooking pans
medium cooking pot

INGREDIENTS:

2 cups	red onions (chopped)
1 cup	oil
1 lb.	fish (dried)
1 lb.	gomen (collard greens)
4 fresh	green peppers (chili Anaheim)
1/4 tsp.	ginger
1/4 tsp.	black pepper
1/4 tsp.	cardamom
to taste	salt
2 cups	water

PREPARATON: Cook *onions* in a pan adding a litle water at a time to *avoid burning*. Add *oil* and continue cooking. Cut dried *fish* into thin pieces and add to the pan. Add 1 cup of *water* and set aside. In a separate pot boil the *greens* after washing and cutting into thin pieces. Squeeze the excess water out of the greens. Add greens to the fish and cook together for 30 minutes. Add *salt*. When ready, remove from the heat, and add *ginger, black pepper* and *cardamom*. Cut and unseed the *green peppers* and add to rest. Serve hot. Makes about 6 servings. Refrigerate to store.

Assa Begomen will make a delicious main course for Lent or fasting. Eat with injera or bread.

FRIED FISH

YE'ASSA T'IBS

UTENSILS: large bowl
large deep frying pan

INGREDIENTS:

6	fish fillets
1 cup	flour (plain)
1 Tbsp.	black pepper
1 cup	oil
to taste	salt

PREPARATION: In a bowl mix *flour* with *black pepper* and *salt*. Roll *fish fillets* in flour. Coat both sides completely. In a deep frying pan bring the *oil* to boil. Add the fish carefully one at a time and fry until brown and crisp. Serve hot. Makes about 6 servings. Cover in foil and refrigerate to store.

Ye'assa T'ibs, Ethiopian style, may also be prepared with whole fish. Cleaned inside and out with water and lemon and fried the same way coated with flour. Serve with a wedge of lemon.

GROUND FISH STEW

YE'ASSA MINCHET ABISH

UTENSILS: medium cooking pan
medium frying pan

INGREDIENTS:

2 cups	dried fish
2 cups	red onions (chopped)
1/4 cup	red pepper (*berbere*)
1/4 cup	oil
1/4 cup	*t'ej* or wine
1 cup	water
1/4 Tbsp.	flax (powdered)
1/4 tsp.	fenugreek
1/4 tsp.	black pepper
to taste	salt

PREPARATION: Cook *red onions* and *flax* at a low heat until it is brown. Add *oil* and *red pepper* stir gently for 15 minutes adding *t'ej* or *wine* a little at a time. In the frying pan fry *dried fish* over a low fire until crisp, pound to a fine powder. Add *fenugreek and powdered fish* to cooking sauce. Add water and simmer gently for 5 minutes. Add *black pepper* and *salt* and stir gently. Serve hot. Makes 6 servings.

Ye'assa Minchet Abish, also served during the fasting period, is very delicious with injera or bread and may be served on special occasions.

HOT FISH STEW

YE'ASSA WE'T

UTENSILS: medium cooking pan
medium frying pan

INGREDIENTS:

3 medium	fish fillets
2 cups	red onions (chopped)
1 cup	oil
1 1/2 cups	water
1/4 cup	red pepper (*berbere*) or red pepper paste (*awaze*)
1/2 cup	*t'ej* or wine
1/4 tsp.	black pepper
to taste	salt

PREPARATION: Cut the *fish fillets* in small pieces and grill without oil in a medium frying pan and set aside. In a separate pan, cook *red onions* until brown. Add *oil* and *red pepper* and stir. Add *t'ej* or *wine*, a little at a time, and keep on stirring. Make sure it does not burn by adding *water* a little at a time, cook sauce for 30 minutes. Add the grilled fish, *black pepper* and *salt* to taste. Cook on low heat for 10 minutes and serve hot. 4-6 servings. Store in refrigerator.

Ye'assa We't is popular during the fasting season or among vegetarians.

RAW FISH

T'IRE ASSA

INGREDIENTS: 3-4   fillet (fresh trout or perch)
1/4 cup   very hot red pepper (*mit'mit'a*)
chili Serrano or red pepper
(*berbere*) or red pepper
paste (*awaze*)

PREPARATION: Wash *fish* and remove skin. Cut fish into medium sized cubes. Serve to room temperature with side dish of *very hot red pepper, red pepper paste* or *red pepper (berbere)* and with injera or bread. Makes about 6 servings. Refrigerate to store.

T'ire Assa (raw fish) like T'ire Siga (raw meat) is simply raw fish eaten with hot pepper as a delicacy. It is also served during Lent (fasting season).

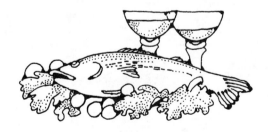

Fish

SLIGHTLY COOKED FISH TARTAR

YE'ASSA IMMIS

UTENSILS: medium mixing bowl
medium pan

INGREDIENTS:

4 medium	fish fillets
1/4 cup	red pepper (*berbere*) or red pepper paste (*awaze*)
1 cup	cooking oil
1/2 cup	*t'ej* or wine
1/4 tsp.	black pepper
2	chopped green peppers (fresh)
to taste	salt

PREPARATION: Cut *fish* into small pieces. Mix *red pepper* or *red pepper paste* with *oil, wine* or *t'ej, salt* and *black pepper*. Chop *green pepper*, add to fish and the red pepper mixture and cook for 5 minutes in low heat. Serve warm. Cover and refrigerate to store. Makes 4-6 servings.

Ye'assa Immis is like Ye'assa Kitfo. Eat with injera or bread.

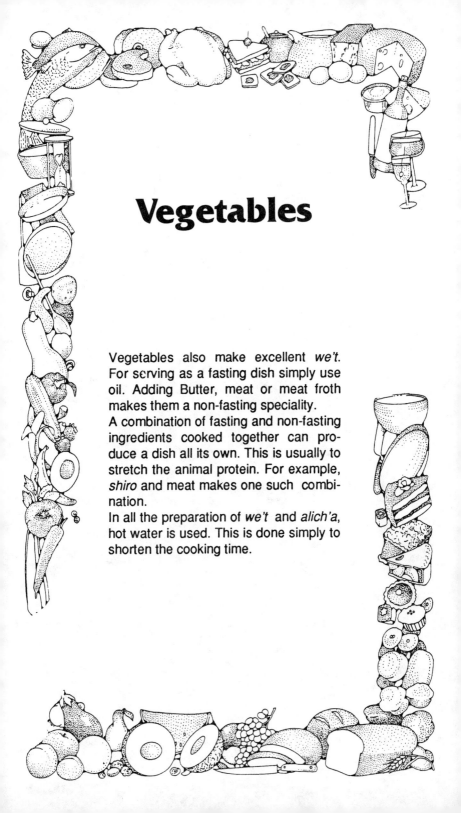

Vegetables

Vegetables also make excellent *we't*. For serving as a fasting dish simply use oil. Adding Butter, meat or meat froth makes them a non-fasting speciality.

A combination of fasting and non-fasting ingredients cooked together can produce a dish all its own. This is usually to stretch the animal protein. For example, *shiro* and meat makes one such combination.

In all the preparation of *we't* and *alich'a*, hot water is used. This is done simply to shorten the cooking time.

BOILED BEETS

YEQEY SIR QIQQIL

UTENSILS: medium cooking pot
mixing bowl

INGREDIENTS: 4   medium beets
to taste   salt
3 Tbsp.   lemon juice
3 Tbsp.   oil
5 cups   water

PREPARATION: Cut leaves and wash *beetroots* thoroughly. In a medium cooking pan add *water* and bring to boil. Reduce heat and simmer for 40 minutes. When *beetroot* feels tender, remove and peel. Cut the *beetroot* either in cubes or slice. Add the *beetroot* in a mixing bowl, mix the *oil* and the *lemon juice* separately, pour over the *beetroot*, and mix.

YEQEY SIR QIQQIL is a vegetarian delight. It may be served for lunch during a hot day either as a side dish or a main course with other vegetables. Carrots are also prepared in similar fashion without oil.

BOILED KALE

ZELBO GOMEN

UTENSILS: medium cooking pan

INGREDIENTS:
1 lb	kale
1 cup	red onions (chopped)
1/2 cup	oil
1 Tbsp	garlic (mashed)
1 Tbsp	ginger (mashed)
4 cups	water
to taste	salt

PREPARATION: Wash *kale* in cold *water*. Tear the leaves from the stem. Peel the stem and cut into small pieces. Add the water to the *kale* and bring to boil. Stir in the *salt, oil, onion, garlic* and *ginger*. Cook until the *kale* is tender for 25 minutes. Serve hot or cold. Serves 6. Refrigerate.

Zelbo Gomen (kale) is the most popular vegetable dish. It is served as a side dish with other food. It is served either cold or warm.

*It is important not to overcook the *kale* to retain the greatest nutritional value. The leaves may also be cooked whole and chopped after cooking.

BOILED SWEET POTATO

YETEQEQQELE SIKWAR DINICH

UTENSILS: large cooking pan
metal brush

INGREDIENTS: 2   large sweet potatoes
15 cups   water

PREPARATION: Wash the *sweet potatoes* in cold water. Scrub the skin lightly with a brush. Add *Sweet potatoes* in 15 cups of *water* and cook for 40 minutes. When tender cool slightly and peel. Serve hot.

Yeteqeqqele Sikwar Dinich may be eaten as a snack or as a dessert. It is delicious and very nourishing. It is very popular among children.

COLLARD GREENS

YE'ABESHA GOMEN

UTENSILS:	medium cooking pan

INGREDIENTS:

1 lb.	collard greens
1 cup	red onions (chopped)
4 medium	green peppers (fresh) sliced in strips (chili Anaheim)
2 cups	water
1/2 tsp.	garlic (peeled and chopped)
16 oz.	butter or oil
to taste	salt

PREPARATION: Wash *collard greens*, boil in medium pan until soft. Remove from heat, drain, and cut into small peices. Set aside. Wash *green peppers*, remove seeds, slice lengthwise and set aside.

In the medium pan, cook *onions* over a low heat until brown adding a little *water* to prevent sticking and burning. Add *oil*. Add collard greens and cook till water disappears. Add all the *spices* and stir gently. One at a time, add the green pepper slices about 10 minutes before removing from fire. Serve hot or cold. Serves 6. Refrigerate.

Ye'abesha Gomen (Collard Greens) is the most delicious vegetable dish. It is served as a side dish with other food. It is served either cold or warm.

COLLARD GREEN WITH MEAT

GOMEN BESIGA

UTENSILS: 2 medium sized cooking pans

INGREDIENTS:
1 lb.	collard greens
1 cup	red onions (chopped)
1/2 lb.	meat with fat
4 medium	green peppers, seeded and sliced (chili Anaheim) or (chili Jalepeño)
2 cups	water
1/2 tsp.	garlic (chopped)
1/2 tsp.	ginger (chopped)
1 cup	butter
to taste	salt

PREPARATION: Wash and boil *collard greens* till soft. Cook *onion* on a separate pan in mild heat for 5 minutes. Add *meat* to the onion and cook till meat is tender. Cut the collard greens in small pieces and add to the meat. Add *butter* and stir. Add the 2 cups of *water* and leave till the meat is done. Add *garlic* and *ginger*, cover pan and let the water evaporate. Wash and unseed green peppers and add in the pan for 10-20 minutes. Remove from heat. Serve hot. Serves 6-8.

Gomen Besiga is a delicious dish served on all occasions.

DRY PUMPKIN SAUCE

YEDUBBA QWANT'A WE'T

UTENSILS: 1 large tray
1 medium cooking pan

INGREDIENTS:
4 cups	pumpkin chopped & dried
2 cups	onions
1 cup	oil
1 Tbsp	red pepper paste (awaze)
1 Tbsp	garlic (mashed)
1 Tbsp	ginger (mashed)
1 tsp	cardamom
1 tsp	black pepper
1/2 cup	tej or white cooking wine
to taste	salt
4 cups	water

PREPARATION: Cut the *pumpkin* in half, remove the seeds and peel. Cut into small cubes, place on a large tray and put in the sun or a dehydrator. Remove any pieces that become moldy.
Cook the onion over a low heat until golden brown, add a little water and stir constantly to prevent sticking. Add the oil and cook for 5 - 10 minutes, stirring occasionally. Add the *awaze* and a little of the water and cook for 20 minutes stirring occasionally. Mix the *garlic, ginger, cardamom, black pepper, tej* or *cooking wine* and *salt* together and then add to the *onion* mixture. Add the *dry pumpkin* and remaining *water*. Cook for 35 minutes. Serve hot or cold. Serves 6. Refrigerate.

Yedubba Qwant'a We't is another vegetarian dish that is eaten with injera or bread. The dry pumpkin is a good substitute for meat. It is believed to have a good quantity of vitamin A & C.

FASTING "CHEESE" FROM POTATOES

YEDINICH BUT'ECHA'

UTENSILS: Medium cooking pan
mixing bowl

INGREDIENTS:

4 medium	potatoes
1/2 cup	oil
1 1/2 cups	green pepper chopped
1 cup	onion chopped
2 Tbsp	lemon juice or vinegar
to taste	salt

PREPARATION: Peel *potatoes* and cut into small pieces.* Cook in 2 cups of *water* for 30 minutes. Discard *water* and mash the *potatoes*. Add the *green peeper, lemon juice, oil* & *salt*. Mix well, refrigerate and keep in cool place before serving.

*The potatoes may be cooked whole & peeled afterwards.

YEDINICH BUT'ECHA' is a vegetarian dish. It is eaten as a substitute for a cottage cheese during the fasting season.

FALSE BANANA DISH

YEQOCH'O MINCHET ABISH

UTENSILS: medium cooking pan

INGREDIENTS:
2 cups	red onions (chopped)
1 cup	butter (spiced)
2 cups	beef with fat (minced)
1/3 cup	red pepper or red pepper paste (*awaze*)
2 cups	qoch'o-bulla (*musaceae*)
1/2 cup	*t'ej* or red wine
1 cup	water
to taste	salt

PREPARATION: Cook *red onions* in *butter* until they are brown. Add *water*. Add minced *meat with fat* and stir until water evaporates. Add *red pepper* (berbere) and *t'ej* or *red wine* and let it simmer until the meat becomes tender. Sift *qoch'o* and sprinkle into mixture and stir. Add *salt* and serve hot. Serves 6. May be refrigerated but it is better to make small amounts and use up right away.

Yeqoch'o Minchet Abish is a dish prepared from the scrapings of the root of a banana-like plant. (It can be prepared without meat. With milk added to it, it is like a porridge or baked like a pan bread. Could be for breakfast, lunch or dinner).

False Banana

170

FRESH GREEN PEPPERS
STUFFED WITH ONION

YEQARYA SINNIG

UTENSILS: serving plate
small mixing bowl

INGREDIENTS: 6 medium   green peppers (chili Jalapeño)
or (chili Anaheim)

                1 cup   ren onions (chopped)
                1/2 cup   oil
                1/4 tsp.   black pepper
                to taste   salt

PREPARATION: Wash *green peppers* in running water. Slice on one side and carefully remove seeds. Put aside. In a mixing bowl add *oil, onions, black pepper* and *salt*, mix well. Stuff the mixtures in the green peppers. Serve fresh. Refrigerate in closed container. Yields 4-6.

Yeqarya Sinnig is green pepper stuffed with onions. It is served with almost all kinds of dishes as a side order.

FRESH TOMATOES AND GREEN PEPPER

TEEMATEEM, BEQARYA

UTENSILS: medium mixing bowl

INGREDIENTS: 3 large   fresh tomatoes
                  4 medium   fresh chiles (green pepper)
                               (chili Anaheim)
                  1/4 cup   red onions (chopped)
                  4 Tbsp.   vegetable oil
                  4 tsp.   lemon juice or vinegar
                  to taste   salt
                  1/4 tsp.   black pepper

PREPARATION: Wash *tomatoes* and chop into very small pieces. Chop *green peppers* after removing the seeds. Add *oil, salt, black pepper, lemon juice* and *onions* to the bowl and mix well. Add chopped tomatoes to the mixture and toss gently but well. Serve cold. Serves 6. Refrigerate mixture in closed container.

Teemateem, Beqarya is a very cool and refreshing vegetarian dish. It may be eaten with bread or injera.

Tomatoes

172

MUSHROOM SAUCE

INGUDAI WE'T

UTENSILS: 1 large cooking pot
2 medium cooking pans

INGREDIENTS:

2 cups	red onions (chopped)
2 cups	mushrooms (ingudai)
1 cup	split peas
1 cup	oil
5 cups	water
1/4 cup	red pepper (*berbere*)
1/4 tsp.	fenugreek
1/2 tsp.	flax
1/2 cup	*t'ej* or wine
1/4 tsp.	black pepper
to taste	salt

PREPARATION: Cook *onions* without grease in a large cooking pan until light brown at edges. Add *fenugreek* and *flax*. Add *oil*, stir well. Add *red pepper* and simmer in a low heat. In the second pan boil the *mushrooms* in 2 cups water, drain and put aside. In third pan boil the split peas in 2 cups water. Add the cooked *peas* with its water into the cooking sauce and stir well. Add the drained mushrooms into the sauce, stir gently and add *spices*. Add *t'ej* or *wine* and the remaining water and cook for 10 minutes and remove from heat. Serve hot or cold. Makes 6 servings. Store in refrigerator. Sautee mushrooms instead of boiling for variety.

Ingudai We't is a seasonal vegetarian dish, delicious when eaten with injera or bread.

OKRA MILD SAUCE

BAMYA ALICH'A

UTENSILS: 1 medium cooking pan

INGREDIENTS:

4 cups	okra (split)
2 cups	onions (chopped)
1 cup	oil
1 1/2 cups	tomatoes (peeled & chopped)
1 Tbsp	garlic (mashed)
1 Tbsp	ginger (mashed)
to taste	salt
1 tsp	cardamom
4 medium	fresh chiles
	(green pepper chopped)
	(chile jalapeño or chili Anaheim)
5 cups	water

PREPARATION: Cut the ends from the *okra*, split in half and soak in 5 cups of *water* overnight. Drain and rinse several times in cold water.

In the medium pan, cook *onions* over a low heat until golden brown, adding a little *water* to prevent sticking and burning. Add *oil* and cook for 5-10 minutes.Add the *tomatoes* and bring to boil. Add the *garlic, ginger, cardamom & salt*; stir well. Add the *okra* and cook for 25 minutes. Add the *green pepper* 4 minutes before removing from heat. serve hot or cold. Serves 6. Refrigerate.

Bamya Alich'a is a vegetarian delight. It is usually served during Lent. It is eaten with injera or bread.

POTATO STEW

DINICH WE'T

UTENSILS: 1 large frying pan
1 medium cooking pot

INGREDIENTS:

2 cups	red onions (chopped)
1 lb.	beef
1 cup	red pepper (*berbere*) or red pepper paste *awaze*)
4 medium	potatoes
1 cup	oil or butter
1/4 tsp.	black pepper
to taste	salt
1/4 tsp.	ginger
1/4 tsp.	garlic
1/2 tsp.	water

PREPARATION: Brown *red onions* in cooking pan by adding a little water at a time. Add *red pepper* and *oil* or *butter*. Add *meat* after cutting into large cubes. While onions and meat mixture is simmering, peel and cut *potatoes* into large pieces and fry in oil in large frying pan. Add potatoes to the meat and onion mixture for a few minutes, stirring until mixed. Heat thoroughly. Serve hot if cooked with butter and meat or cold if cooked with oil. Makes 6 servings. Refrigerate.

Dinich We't may be vegetarian or served at anytime with meat and injera or bread.

PUMPKIN SAUCE

YEDUBBA WE'T

UTENSILS: 1 medium cooking pot

INGREDIENTS:
4 cups	pumpkin, cubed
1 cup	onions (chopped)
1 tsp	garlic (mashed)
1 cup	oil
1/2 cup	red pepper
1/4 tsp	black cumin
to taste	salt
1/4 tsp	garlic & ginger powder
5 cups	water

PREPARATION: Brown *onions* in cooking pan, stirring constantly, and adding a little boiling water at a time to prevent sticking. Add the *oil* and cook for 5-10 minutes, stirring constantly. Add the *red pepper*, black *cumin* and salt and cook for 20 more minutes, stirring occasionally, and adding a little of the boiling water as needed to prevent sticking.

Add the peeled and *cubed pumpkin* and bring to boil. Add the garlic and *ginger* powder and the remaining water. Cook until the *pumpkin* is tender. Serve hot. Makes 6 servings. Store in refrigerator.

Yedubba We't is a vegetarian dish. Delicious when eaten with injera or bread.

PUMPKIN MILD SAUCE

YEDUBBA ALICH'A

UTENSILS: 1 medium cooking pot

INGREDIENTS:
4 cups	pumpkin (cubed)
1 cup	oil
1 cup	onions (chopped)
1 tsp	garlic (mashed)
1 tsp	ginger (mashed)
1/4 tsp	turmeric
to taste	salt
4 medium	fresh chilies (green pepper chopped)

PREPARATION: Cook *onion* over a low heat until golden brown stirring constantly and adding a little *water* at times to prevent sticking. Add the oil and the *turmeric*. Cook for 5-10 minutes stirring occasionally. Add the *garlic, ginger* and the remaining water and bring to boil. Add the *pumpkin* and cook for 20 minutes until the pumpkin is tender. Remove the seeds from the *green peppers* and chop into large pieces. Add the green pepper 4 minutes before removing from heat. Serve hot or cold. Store in refrigerator. Makes about 4 servings.

Yedubba Alich'a is another vegetarian dish which is a good source of vitamin A & C. It is eaten with injera or bread.

PUREED GREEN LENTILS
HARMONIOUSLY BLENDED WITH SPICES

AZIFA

UTENSILS: medium mixing bowl
cooking pot

INGREDIENTS:

1 1/2 cups	lentils
3 medium	limes (juice from)
to taste	salt
5 medium	green peppers (chili Anaheim)
3 medium	red onions (chopped)
1/2 tsp.	black pepper
1/2 tsp.	ginger powder
1 cup	cooking oil
1 Tbsp.	English mustard

PREPARATION: Wash and boil *lentils* until they are soft. Drain the water and mash. Seed *green peppers* and cut them and the *onions* into small pieces. Mix the mashed lentils with *oil, mustard* and *lime juice*. Then add the green peppers, onions, *ginger, salt* and *black pepper*. Mix well and refrigerate. Serve cold as needed. Azifa will not keep for too long. Yields 6-8 servings.

Azifa is a vegetarian dish usually served during Lent. It is eaten with injera or bread or can be served with lettuce and tomatoes and cottage cheese for a light, diet snack.

SPINACH LIKE PLANT SAUCE "NETTLE"

SAMMA WE'T

UTENSILS: medium cooking pan
strainer

INGREDIENTS: 2 lbs.   sama leaves (Nettle) (Ortiche)
1 cup   barley powder
1/4 tsp.   garlic (fresh minced)
to taste   salt
2 cups   water

PREPARATION: Rub *sama* leaves through a sieve, chop, put in
boiling water and cook. When done, remove,
drain in strainer and set aside. Place drained
sama and *barley powder* in a bowl, mix together well and add a little warm *water* until
the mixture gets thin. Add garlic and pour the
mixture slowly in a sauce pan and cook for 10-
15 minutes stirring rapidly to prevent lumping.
When done, add *salt*, remove from heat, pour
into bowl and cook before serving. Makes
about 6 servings. Refrigerate.

Samma is made on very rare occasions and only during Lent. It
is made from a hairy, leafy shrub which grows wild and stings
the skin when touched. Use of rubber or plastic gloves will prevent skin irritation. It looks like spinach after it has been cooked.

Nettle

VEGETABLE STEW

YE'ATAKILT ALICH'A

UTENSILS: medium cooking pan

INGREDIENTS:

1 1/2 cups	oil
1 1/2 cups	red onions (chopped)
6 medium	potatoes
5 medium	carrots
1 small can	tomato paste
1 small	cabbage
6 medium	green peppers (chili Anaheim)
1/4 tsp.	garlic powder
to taste	salt
1/4 tsp.	black pepper

PREPARATION: Cook *onions* in *oil* in a medium pan *without browning*. Add *tomato paste* and mix well. Set aside. Peel and slice carrots. Wash and cut *cabbage* into large pieces. Add carrots and cabbage to frying onions. Stir gently and cook until tender. Peel and cut potatoes and add to the mixture. Add *garlic powder* and cook 30-45 minutes. Season to taste with *salt* and *black pepper*. Just before serving, slice *green peppers* lengthwise and dip into the sauce. Serve hot or cold. Makes 6 servings. Refrigerate to store.

Variations: Substitute *cauliflower* or *broccoli* for cabbage and leave out potatoes. Use bell peppers instead of hot green peppers to keep sauce mild and add a little turmeric to color. Freshly made ginger and garlic paste give excellent flavor.

Ye'atakilt Alich'a makes a tasty vegetarian dish with injera or bread and side orders of split pea sauce or lentil sauce.

Legumes

The cooking procedure and the basic ingredients of all the different *we'ts* are the same. The previous type, *qey we't*, and *alich'a* can be prepared from meat, legumes and vegetables. The major difference between the *qey we't,* so-called because of the *berbere* added for flavor and turmeric *(Curcuna longa)* for coloring. The green pepper is cut into strips and the seeds removed before adding it into the sauce, but only during the last few minutes before serving, which is enough time to blend it with the other ingredients.

Such process preserves the vitamin C in the pepper.

Alich'a is always used as a second dish eaten, like all other Ethiopian dishes, with *injera*.

On the other hand, *we't* prepared from peas, chick peas, lentils, broad beans and other plant life makes a fasting dish. Fasting dishes can be made into non-fasting fares by simply using butter instead of oil in the cooking process.

BROAD BEANS FLOUR
MIXED WITH SUN FLOWER WATER

ILBET

UTENSILS: 2 medium cooking pans
medium mixing bowl
deep serving bowl
mortar and pestle
strainer

INGREDIENTS:
1 cup	broad beans
1 cup	sun flower seeds
2 Tbsp.	oil
1 tsp.	garlic
1 tsp.	ginger
5 cups	water
to taste	salt

PREPARATION: Boil *sun flower seeds* in 3 cups of *water* for 5-10 minutes. Discard water and pound sunflower seeds. In a mixing bowl add the pounded sun flower seeds and 2 cups of water and rub by hand. When mixture is slightly thick strain. Keep sun flower water in a bowl and discard the seed. In a medium cooking pan boil 1 cup of *broad beans* with the sun flower seeds water in low heat for 5 minutes adding 2 Tbsp. *oil* and stir well. Put mixture in a deep serving bowl and add *garlic, ginger, salt* and mix well until smooth. Store in refrigerator covered. Serve cold. Serves 6-12.

Ilbet is a delicious dish eaten with injera or bread.

CHICK PEA PASTE

BUT'ECHA'

UTENSILS: medium pan
mixing bowl

INGREDIENTS: 2 cups   powdered chick peas or lentils
1/2 cup   oil
1 cup   red onion (chopped)
1 Tbsp.   mustard
2 Tbsp.   lemon juice
1/4 tsp.   black pepper
to taste   salt
1/4 cup   red pepper (*berbere*)
4 cups   green pepper

PREPARATION: Mix *chick pea powder* with *red pepper* in 1 cup
of *water* and cook over low heat for 10-20 min-
utes. Remove from stove and set aside. Blend
green peppers with *red onion, oil, black pepper, mustard, lemon juice* and *salt* to taste. Add
this to the powder mixture, blend well, cook
and serve. Makes 6 servings. Refrigerate.

But'echa' is another variety of a vegetarian dish. It may be
eaten with injera or bread.

CHICK PEA FLOUR CAKES
(IN SHAPES OF FISH)

YESHIMBRA ASSA

UTENSILS: medium cooking pan
large flat baking pan/cookie sheet

INGREDIENTS:

2 cups	water
2 cups	red onions (chopped)
2 cups	chick pea flour
1 1/2 cups	oil
1/2 cup	red pepper (*berbere*)
1/2 tsp.	cardamom
1/4 tsp.	ginger
1/4 tsp.	garlic
to taste	salt

PREPARATION: Cook *onions* in a medium pan until brown. Add 5 Tbsp. *water* and mix. Add *red pepper* and 1 cup *oil* stirring to mix. Add the remaining *water*, mix and cover till the mixture boils. Set aside.

Mix *pea flour* with water in a bowl. Add half of the *oil* and rub between fingers. Preheat oven to 350°. Shape dough in little fish-like figures, place on cookie sheet, and bake until golden brown. Set aside to cool.

Replace the pan of cooking onions on medium heat and add *spices*. Put the chick pea cakes into the pan and stir gently for 15 minutes. Add *salt* to taste. Serve hot. Makes 6 servings. Refrigerate.

This vegetarian delicacy acts as chicken stew during Lent. Eat with injera or bread.

COOKED WHEAT & SPLIT BROAD BEANS

GULBAN

UTENSILS: large cooking pot

INGREDIENTS: 4 cups   wheat flour
                  1 1/2 cups   split broad beans
                  to taste   salt
                  20 cups   water

PREPARATION: In a large cooking pot add the wheat flour and bring to boil, reduce the heat and simmer for about 2-1/2 hours. Add the *salt*, the *broad beans* and cook for 25-30 minutes until the broad beans are tender. When ready remove from heat and serve hot. Serves 6.

Gulban is traditionally eaten on the Thursday before Easter. It is very delicious and filling. Red pepper is tossed in it to give it a hot and spicy flavor.

COTTON SEED SAUCE

YET'IFT'IRE WE'T

UTENSILS: 3 medium cooking pans

INGREDIENTS: 1 cup   cotton seeds (Gossypium sp.)
2 cups   red onions (chopped)
1/2 cup   red pepper (*berbere*) or red
             pepper paste (*awaze*)
1 cup   oil
1 cup   split peas
1/4 tsp. black pepper
to taste salt
4 cups   water

PREPARATION: Boil *cotton seeds* in cold *water*, remove from heat, drain and discard water. Set aside to cool. When it gets cool pound, mix with 1/2 cup *water* and set aside. In another pan cook *onions* with *oil* until brown. Add *berbere* or *awaze* and continue cooking. On the third pan boil *split peas* intwo cups cold water for 20 minutes, drain, discard water and set aside. Add split peas to the cooking onions and stir, making sure the bottom does not stick. Add cotton seeds and water and keep on stirring. Add *salt* and *black pepper* before removing from heat and serve hot. Makes about six servings. Refrigerate.

Yet'ift'ire We't, another vegetarian dish, is prepared on very rare occasions and served with injera.

DRIED BEEF WITH POWDERED PEA SAUCE

YEQWANT'A SHIRO

UTENSILS: medium cooking pan

INGREDIENTS: 4 cups   water
8 oz.   butter (spiced)
1 cup   dried beef
1 cup   spiced pea flour
1/4 tsp.   salt

PREPARATION: Boil *water*. Add *butter*. When butter melts, lower heat, add *spiced pea flour*, small amounts at a time, stirring constantly so lumps won't form. Add *dried meat* and simmer gently for about 45 minutes. Serve hot with injera or bread. Makes 6 servings. Refrigerate.

When you run out of meat and you don't have too much time to create a fantastic meal **Yeqwant'a Shiro** is the simplest meal to prepare.

HOT PEA FLOUR SAUCE

YESHIRO WE'T

UTENSILS: medium cooking pan

INGREDIENTS:

1 1/2 cups	spiced powdered peas
2 cups	water
1 cup	red onions (chopped)
1 1/2 cups	oil
to taste	salt
1/4 tsp.	garlic
4	green peppers (optional) (chili Anaheim)

PREPARATION: Fry *onions* with *oil* in pan until brown. Add *water* and let it boil. Sprinkle *spiced powdered peas* a little at a time, stirring to prevent lumps. Add *spices* and cook until sauce is smooth and thick. Add *green pepper* slices to sauce and remove from heat. Serve hot or cold. Warm slowly over heat. Yields 6-8 servings. Refrigerate.

Yeshiro We't is a spicier and mildly hot version of Yeshiro Alich'a. It is finger licking good. Very popular for any occasion.

MILD PEA FLOUR SAUCE

YESHIRO ALICH'A

UTENSILS: medium cooking pan

INGREDIENTS: 1 1/2 cups mildly spiced powdered peas
2 cups   water
1 cup   red onions (chopped)
1 1/2 cups   oil
to taste   salt
4   green peppers (fresh) sliced
             lengthwise, seeds removed
             (chili Anaheim)
1/4 tsp.   garlic

PREPARATION: Fry *onions* with *oil* in pan. Add *water* and let it boil. Sprinkle *pea flour* a little at a time, stirring to prevent lumps. Add *spices* and cook until sauce is smooth and thick. Add *green peppers* to sauce and remove from heat. Serve hot or cold. Warm on low heat. Makes 6 servings. Refrigerate.

Yeshiro Alich'a, another vegetarian dish, is prepared almost regularly as a fast food for breakfast, lunch or dinner. Good with injera or bread.

MILD SPLIT PEA SAUCE

YEKIK ALICH'A

UTENSILS: 2 medium cooking pans

INGREDIENTS:

2 cups	split peas (red or green)
4 cups	water
2 cups	red onions (chopped)
2 cups	oil
1 Tbsp.	ginger
1 Tbsp.	garlic
4	green peppers (fresh) (chili Anaheim) or (chili Jalepeño)
to taste	salt
1 tsp.	black pepper

PREPARATION: Wash *split peas* and boil until soft. Remove peas, drain, and reserve water for later use. In the medium pan, cook *onions* with *oil*, stirring gently. Add cooked peas and stir to prevent sticking to bottom of pan. Add *garlic, ginger* and *black pepper* and continue to simmer for 20-30 minutes, stirring occasionally. Slice *green pepper* and add to sauce. Serve hot or cold. Makes 6 servings. Refrigerate.

Yekik Alich'a is a milder version of Yikik We't. Cooked with oil it is also a vegetarian dish eaten during Lent. When Yikik Alich'a is prepared with oil serve hot or cold. If it is prepared with butter serve hot.

191

PEA FLOUR PASTE

INFIRFIR SHIRO

UTENSILS: medium cooking pan

INGREDIENTS:
1 cup	red onions (chopped)
1 1/2 cups	oil
1/3 cup	red pepper (*berbere*) or red pepper paste (*awaze*)
2 cups	pea flour
1/4 tsp.	cardamom
1/2 tsp.	ginger
to taste	salt
1/2 tsp.	garlic
2 1/2 cups	water

PREPARATION: Brown *onions* with *oil* in a medium pan. Add 1/2 cup of *water* and stir. Add *red pepper paste* or *red pepper*, stirring gently. Add 2 more cups of water and cook until water boils. Sprinkle the *pea flour* into the mixture stirring to prevent lumps. Add *spices* and *salt* as needed. Serve hot or cold. Serves 6. Refrigerate.

Infirfir Shiro is a thick paste-like sauce. May be eaten with injera or spread on bread and served as snacks or appetizer.

PEA FLOUR SAUCE

BOZENA SHIRO

UTENSILS: medium cooking pan

INGREDIENTS: 1 cup   red onions (chopped)
1 1/2 lbs.   beef (ground)
1 cup   butter (spiced)
1 cup   spiced hot powdered peas or
mildly spiced powdered peas
1/4 tsp.   ginger
1/2 tsp.   false cardamom
to taste   salt
2 cups   water

PREPARATION: Cook *red onions* in *butter*. Add 2 cups *water* and stir gently. When water boils, add *meat* and mix well. Add *pea flour* while stirring, to prevent lumping. Add *ginger* and *false cardamom* and cook until butter rises up to the surface. Serve hot. Enough for 6 servings. Store in refrigerator.

Bozena Shiro is a favorite dish among many. It is tasty with injera, served preferably hot, at every meal.

SPLIT BROAD BEAN SAUCE

YEBAQELA KIK WE'T

UTENSILS: large cooking pan
medium cooking pan

INGREDIENTS:

2 cups	split broad beans (dried)
6 cups	water (boiled)
2 cups	red onions (chopped)
1 1/2 cups	oil
1 Tbsp.	garlic (mashed)
1 cup	red pepper (berbere)
to taste	salt
1/4 tsp.	black cumin

INGREDIENTS: Wash *broad beans* and boil in 4 cups of *water* for 5 minutes (until the broad beans are tender) save water for later use.

In a medium pan cook onions over a low heat until golden brown, adding a little water as needed to prevent sticking. Add the *oil* and cook for 5 - 10 minutes. Add the *berbere*, *black cumin*, and *salt*. Cook for 15 minutes stirring occasionally and adding a little water as needed to prevent sticking.

Add the *beans* and the liquid in which they were cooked. Add the garlic and bring to boil, reduce heat and simmer for 30 minutes. Makes 6 or more serving.

Yebaqela Kik We't is split broad beans, a favorite dish among many vegetarian lovers.

194

SPLIT PEA SAUCE WITH MEAT & BONES

DOYYO

UTENSILS: medium cooking pan

INGREDIENTS:
1 cup	red onions (chopped)
1 cup	buter (spiced)
1 tsp.	ginger (powder)
1/4 tsp.	garlic (powder)
1/2 tsp.	false cardamom
1 cup	pea flour
1/2 cup	red pepper (*berbere*)
to taste	salt
1 lb.	meat with bones
6 cups	water

PREPARATION: Cook *red onions* in pan until brown. Add *meat* and 4 cups of *water*. Add *ginger, garlic, red pepper* and *pea flour* a little at a time, stirring to avoid lumps. If sauce is too thin add a little water and stir. Simmer, stirring occasionally for 15 minutes, remove from heat and serve hot. Makes 6 servings. Refrigerate.

Doyyo is sort of an everyday dish which could be prepared from leftover meat or without. Best eaten with injera or bread.

SPLIT LENTIL SAUCE

YEMISIR KIK WE'T

UTENSILS: large cooking pan
medium cooking pan

INGREDIENTS:

2 cups	split lentils (dried)
6 cups	water (boiled)
2 cups	red onions (chopped)
1 1/2 cups	oil
1 Tbsp.	ginger
1 tsp.	garlic
1 cup	red pepper (berbere)
1/4 tsp.	black cumin

PREPARATION: Wash *lentils* and boil for 5 minutes (until the lentils are tender). Cook onions adding *oil* and stirring gently until golden brown adding a little *water* as needed to prevent sticking. Remove lentils from heat, drain and reserve water for later use. Add the *lentils* to the *onions*. Add reserved water stirring to prevent mixture from sticking to the bottom of the pan. Add *red pepper*, *ginger*, *garlic*, *black cumin* and *salt* to taste. Simmer for 20 minutes, 6 or more servings. Refrigerate.

Yemisir Kik We't is a spicier and mildly hot version of Yemisir Kik Alich'a.

SPLIT LENTIL SAUCE (MILD)

YEMISIR ALICH'A

UTENSILS: large cooking pan
medium cooking pan

INGREDIENTS:

2 cups	split lentils
6 cups	water
2 cups	red onions (chopped)
2 cups	oil or butter
1 Tbsp.	ginger
1 tsp.	garlic
4 fresh	green peppers (sliced length-wise) (chili Anaheim)
1/4 tsp.	black pepper
to taste	salt

PREPARATION: Wash *lentils* and boil for 5 minutes. Cook *onions* adding *oil* and stirring gently so onions won't turn brown. Remove lentils from the heat, drain and reserve water for later use. Add lentils to the onions. Add reserved water, stirring to prevent mixture from sticking to the bottom of the pan. Add *spices* and *salt* to taste. Simmer for another 20 minutes. 6 or more servings. Refrigerate.

Yemisir Alich'a is similar to Yikik Alich'a and is yet another delicious vegetarian dish. Serve with injera or bread.

SPLIT PEA SAUCE

YEKIK WE'T

UTENSILS: 2 medium cooking pans

INGREDIENTS:

2 cups	split peas (red)
2 cups	red onions (chopped)
2 cups	oil
4 cups	water
1/3 cup	red cooking wine
1$ tsp.	ginger
1/4 tsp.	fenugreek
1 cup	red pepper (*berbere*)
to taste	salt
1/2 cup	red wine or *t'ej*

PREPARATION: Wash *split peas* and boil until soft, about 15-20 minutes. Drain water from peas, set them aside, save water. Cook *onion* and *fenugreek* until brown and soft, using a little of the water at a time to prevent burning. Add *red pepper* and stir. Add 1 1/2 cups more of the reserved water. Add *oil* and *salt* and stir well. Add cooked split peas and *red wine* or *t'ej*. Sprinkle in *spices*. Add remaining water and cook for 15 minutes. Remove from heat, and serve hot or cold. Serves 6. Refrigerate.

Yekik We't is also a vegetarian dish which is prepared with oil for Lent and with butter and sometimes meat for a delicious lunch or dinner with injera or bread. When Yekik We't is prepared with oil you can serve hot or cold, but when it is prepared with butter serve hot.

SPICED CHICK PEA BREAD

YESHIMBRA KITFO

UTENSILS: medium cooking pan
medium mixing bowl
flat tray

INGREDIENTS:
1 cup	red onions (chopped)
1/4 cup	red pepper (*berbere*)
2 cups	chick pea powder
4	green peppers chopped (fresh) (chili Jalapeño)
1/4 tsp.	black pepper
1/2 cup	oil
to taste	salt
1	lemon (squeezed)
1 cup	water

PREPARATION: Mix *chick pea powder* and *red pepper* and cook over low fire, adding small amounts of *water* at a time, stirring constantly. Transfer mixture to a flat tray and leave for about 15 minutes to dry. Add a little *oil* and roll to a pizza crust thickness and cool. Break into litle pieces and set aside.

Mix chopped *green peppers* with *onions*, remaining oil, *lemon juice, salt* and *black pepper*. Add these to the chick peas; mix and serve cold. Makes 6 servings. Refrigerate.

Yeshimbra Kitfo is a very unusual vegetarian dish which makes a tasty salad.

WHOLE DRIED PEA SAUCE

YEDIFIN ATER ALICH'A

UTENSILS: medium cooking pan

INGREDIENTS: 1 1/2 cups   whole dried peas
2 cups   red onions (chopped)
1 1/2 cups   oil
3 cups   water
1/4 tsp.   garlic
1/2 tsp.   ground ginger
3 medium   green peppers (fresh) sliced
               lengthwise, seeds removed
               (chili Anaheim)
to taste   salt

PREPARATION: Cook *onions* lightly in a medium pan, stirring constantly so the color doesn't change. Add *oil*. Add *water*. Add *peas* and bring to boil. Add *garlic* and *ginger* and more water. Cook until peas get soft. Add *green pepper* slices to sauce. Add *salt* to taste. Serve hot. Makes 6 servings. Refrigerate.

Yedifin Ater Alich'a is yet another vegetarian dish, mild and nourishing. Serve with injera pieces added to the sauce.

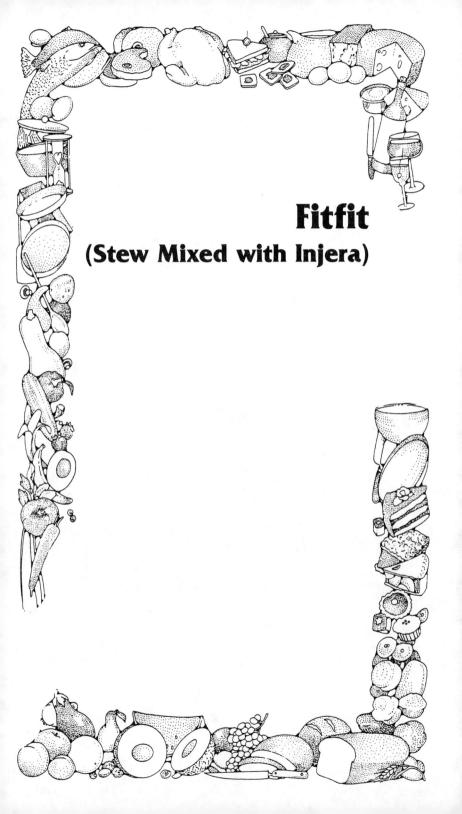

Fitfit
(Stew Mixed with Injera)

FLAX WATER MIXED WITH INJERA

TELBA FITFIT

UTENSILS: medium cooking pan
medium mixing bowl
mortar and pestle

INGREDIENTS:

1 cup	flax seeds (dry)
1 tsp.	red pepper (*berbere*)
to taste	salt
3-4 cups	water
3-4 pieces	Injera
1/4 tsp.	cinnamon

PREPARATION: Roast *flax* seeds in pan at low heat for 5-10 minutes. Remove from heat and let cool. Pound roasted flax to fine powder using mortar and pestle. Add *cinnamon, red pepper (berbere), salt,* and *water* to powder and mix well. Break *injera* into small pieces and add to the flax water. Refrigerate. Serve cold. Yields 4-6 servings. Powder should be stored in closed jar.

Telba Fitfit is a refreshing meal for a hot day or after fasting. May act as a mild laxative.

FRESH CHOPPED TOMATOES BLENDED IN SPICES AND INJERA

TEEMATEEM FITFIT

UTENSILS: medium mixing bowl
covered jar or bottle

INGREDIENTS:

3 medium	ripe tomatoes
2 lmedium	red onions (chopped)
10 medium	green peppers (chili Jalapeño)
2 Tbsp.	red pepper (*berbere*) or red pepper paste (*awaze*)
1/2 cup	oil
juice of 2	lemons (fresh)
1 cup	white wine or *t'ej*
4 fresh	injeras
to taste	salt
1/4 tsp.	black pepper
1/4 tsp.	garlic
3 cups	water

PREPARATION: Peel *tomatoes* (immerse in boiling water for 1 to 2 minutes—skins peel off easily). Chop tomatoes into very small pieces. Chop *green peppers* after removing the seeds. Chop *red onions*. In a separate bowl mix *red pepper* or *red pepper paste* with *wine*. Add tomatoes, onions, peppers and *oil, garlic, black pepper, salt, lemon juice* to the bowl. Mix well. Break *injera* into small pieces and add to mixture until vegetables absorb moisture. When moist, serve cold. Serves 6. Refrigerate mixture in bottle or jar.

Teemateem Fitfit is a very cool and refreshing meal suitable for summer when one doesn't feel like cooking. The mixture may be eaten with bread also.

Fitfit (Stew Mixed with Injera)

INJERA IN SAUCE MIXED OVER LOW FIRE

GINFILFIL

UTENSILS: medium cooking pan

INGREDIENTS:

4 fresh	injera
1 lb.	beef (minced)
2 cups	red onions (chopped)
3/4 cup	red pepper (*berbere*)
1 1/2 cups	butter (spiced)
1/4 cup	powdered peas
1 Tbsp.	fenugreek
1 1/2 Tbsp.	ginger
1/2 tsp.	cardamom
1/4 tsp.	bishop's weed
1/4 tsp.	garlic
1/4 tsp.	cinnamon
1/4 tsp.	black pepper
to taste	salt
3 cups	water
1/2 cup	wine (cooking)

PREPARATION: Cook *red onions* until brown in pan. Add *fenugreek*. Add 1/2 cup *water* and *berbere* and stir. Add *wine*. Add *meat* and mix well. When water has evaporated add *butter*. Cook well, stirring gently. Add 1 cup of water and *powdered peas* continue stirring. When sauce is thick, add remainder of water a little at a time and continue stirring until sauce is thick. Add *spices*, stirring to mix. Break *injera* into pieces; add to sauce; simmer gently for about 2 minutes and serve hot. Serves 6. Refrigerate sauce. Bread may be substituted for injera.

Ginfilfil is a favorite breakfast dish which may be served at other meals. It can also be prepared with left over meat sauce or chick sauces.

NIGERSEED MIXED WITH INJERA

YENUG FITFIT

UTENSILS: strainer
medium mixing bowl
frying pan
mortar and pestle

INGREDIENTS: 1/2 cup   Nigerseed
to taste   salt
1 cup   water
2 pieces   injera

PREPARATION: *Nigerseed presscake:-* Remove all foreign material from seeds. Spread over a large tray and leave in the sun to dry. Toast the dried nigerseed until golden brown in a frying pan stirring constantly. Pound in a clean dry mortar until the nigerseeds become sticky. Press between the palms of the hands to form presscake.
Mix the *nigerseed presscake*, salt & water together. Strain through a sieve. Discard the solid after straining.
In a mixing bowl, tear *injera* into small pieces. Add the liquid and stir until liquid is absorbed into the injera. If too much liquid, add more injera. If too dry add more liquid. Serve cold. Refrigerate to store. Makes 4 serving.

Yenug Fitfit is a refreshing meal for a hot day or after fasting. It may act as a mild laxative.

SESAME MIXED WITH INJERA

YESELIT' FITFIT

UTENSILS: medium mixing bowl
mortar and pastle
medium frying pan

INGREDIENTS:

1/2 cup	sesame
to taste	salt
1 cup	water
2 pieces	injera

PREPARATION: Sesame presscake:- Remove all foreign material from seeds. Spread over a large tray and leave in the sun to dry. Toast the dried *sesame seeds* until golden brown in a frying pan. Stir constantly. Pound in a clean dry mortar until the *sesame seeds* become sticky. Press between the palms of the hands to form presscakes.

Mix the *sesame presscake*, *salt* and *water* together in meedium mixing bowl. Strain through a sieve. Discard the solid after straining.

In a mixing bowl, tear *injera* into small pieces. Add the liquid and stir until liquid is absorbed into the injera. If too much liquid, add more injera. If too dry add more liquid. Serve cold. Refrigerate to store. Makes 4 serving.

Yeseli't Fitfit is a refreshing meal by itself. It is mild and nourishing.

PEA FLOUR DISSOLVED IN WATER AND MIXED IN INJERA

YESHIRO FITFIT

UTENSILS: serving bowl

INGREDIENTS:
1/2 cup	powdered peas (spiced)
2-3 cups	water
1 Tbsp.	onion (chopped)
2 Tbsp.	oil (cooking)
2 Tbsp.	wine (white)
3 fresh	green pepper (diced) (chili Jalapeño)
3-4	injera
to taste	salt

PREPARATION: Add *powdered peas* in bowl. Add *water* and make sure the powder dissolves well, no lumps. Add all the *remaining ingredients*. Cut *injera* into small pieces and add to bowl and make sure the injera is soaked well. Serve cold. Yields 4-6 servings. Refrigerate if mixed with injera.

Yeshiro Fitfit makes a refreshing fast meal to be served on a hot day. Also popular during Lent.

SUNFLOWER WATER MIXED WITH INJERA

YESUFF FITFIT

UTENSILS: medium cooking pot
medium bowl
strainer
blender

INGREDIENTS:
2 cups	sunflower seeds
2 cups	green pepper (chopped) (chili Jalapeño)
1/2 tsp.	onion (chopped)
1/4 tsp.	ginger (chopped)
1/4 tsp.	garlic (chopped)
to taste	salt
10 cups	water
4-6 slices	Injera

PREPARATION: Boil *sunflower seeds* at high temperature in 6 cups of water for 15 minutes. Remove from heat and drain off liquid. Grind seeds in a blender until they turn to a paste. Put paste in medium bowl and add 4 cups of cold water. Mix and strain, pour liquid in bowl and discard the paste. Add *onions, ginger, green pepper* to the liquid. Mix well and *salt* to taste. Break *injera* into small pieces and add to the liquid. Make sure that the injera is well soaked. Refrigerate. Serve cold in a bowl. Makes 4-6 servings.

Yesuff Fitfit is a delicious and refreshing meal especially good for Lent.

Fitfit (Stew Mixed with Injera)

WHOLE BROAD BEANS BLENDED IN SPICES AND INJERA

YEBAQELA FITFIT

UTENSILS: medium cooking pan
medium serving bowl

INGREDIENTS:

1 1/2 cups	whole dried beans
2 cups	red onions (chopped)
1 1/2 cups	oil
4 cups	water
1/4tsp.	garlic
1/2 tsp.	ground ginger
1/4 tsp.	black pepper
3 medium	green peppers sliced length-wise with seeds removed (fresh) (chili Anaheim)
to taste	salt
4 medium	injera

PREPARATION: Cook *onions* lightly in a medium pan, stirring constantly so the color doesn't change. Add *oil*, 2 cups of *water*. Add *broad beans* bring to boil for 5-10 minutes. Add *garlic* and *ginger* and 2 cups *water*. Cook until peas get soft. Add *green pepper* and *salt*. Cut *injera* into small pieces and add to bowl and make sure the injera is soaked well. Serve hot or cold. Yields 4-6. Refrigerate if mixed with injera.

Yebaqela Fitfit is a refreshing meal by itself. It is mild and nourishing.

WHOLE DRIED CHICK PEA SAUCE BLENDED IN SPICES AND INJERA

YESHIMBRA FITFIT

UTENSILS: medium cooking pan
medium serving bowl

INGREDIENTS:

1 1/2 cups	whole dried chick peas
2 cups	red onions (chopped)
1 1/2 cups	oil
4 cups	water
1/4 tsp.	garlic
1/2 tsp.	ground ginger
1/4 tsp.	black pepper
3 medium	green peppers sliced length-wise with seeds removed (fresh) (chili Anaheim)
to taste	salt
4 medium	injera

PREPARATON: Cook *onions* lightly in a medium pan, stirring constantly so the color doesn't change. Add *oil, 2 cups of water*. Add *chick peas* bring to boil for 5-10 minutes. Add *garlic, ginger* and 2 cups *water*. Cook until peas get soft. Add *green pepper* and *salt*. Cut *injera* into small pieces and add to bowl and make sure the injera is soaked well. Serve hot or cold. Yields 4-6. Refrigerate if mixed with injera.

Yeshimbra Fitfit is a refreshing meal by itself. It is mild and nourishing.

Fitfit (Stew Mixed with Injera)

WHOLE DRIED PEA SAUCE BLENDED IN SPICES AND INJERA

YE'ATER FITFIT

UTENSILS: medium cooking pan
medium serving bowl

INGREDIENTS:

1 1/2 cups	whole dried peas
2 cups	red onions (chopped)
1 1/2 cups	oil
4 cups	water
1/4 tsp.	garlic
1/2 tsp.	ground ginger
1/4 tsp.	black pepper
3 medium	green peppers sliced length-wise with seeds removed (fresh) (chili Anaheim)
to taste	salt
4 medium	injera

PREPARATION: Cook *onions* lightly in a medium pan, stirring constantly so the color doesn't change. Add *oil*, 2 cups of *water*. Add *peas* and bring to boil for 5-10 minutes. Add *garlic* and *ginger* and 2 cups of water. Cook until peas get soft. Add *green pepper* and *salt* to taste. Cut *injera* into small pieces and add to bowl and make sure the injera is soaked well. Serve hot or cold. Yields 4-6. Refrigerate if mixed with injera.

Ye'ater Fitfit is a refreshing meal by itself. It is mild and nourishing.

Breakfast

BARLEY OR WHEAT PORRIDGE

GENFO

UTENSILS: deep cooking pot
small serving bowls

INGREDIENTS:

2 cups	corn, barley or wheat flour
4 cups	water
to taste	salt
1/2 cup	butter or oil
1 Tbsp.	red pepper (*berbere*) or red pepper paste (*awaze*)

PREPARATION: Boil *water*, some *butter* or *oil* and *salt* together in a deep pot. Place half of the liquid in a bowl for later use. Add *barley* or *wheat flour* to remaining liquid on stove, sprinkling it and stirring constantly to avoid lumps. When the mixture thickens, add a little water from the bowl and keep stirring until it resembles a smooth, thick butter. Remove from heat and serve in small bowls. Form a well in the center. Add a mixture of *red pepper* and left-over oil or butter. Eat by dipping genfo into mixture using spoon. Serves 6. May be immediately refrigerated but most tasteful when served immediately.

Genfo is a breakfast favorite. Popular among expectant and new mothers.

CEREAL BUTTER

AJJA

UTENSILS: medium mixing bowl
2 medium pans
strainer

INGREDIENTS:

2 cups	crushed wheat, barley or oats
4 cups	water
14 oz.	butter (spiced)
to taste	salt
2 cups	milk
3-4 Tbsp.	sugar

PREPARATION: Soak *cereal* for about 12 hours in cold *water*. Rub with your hands, to remove lumps and strain into a pan. Cover and let stand until the water separates leaving the cereal at the bottom. Drain off the water carefully. In another pan, boil *milk* and *butter* over a low heat and add cereal to it, stirring constantly to avoid lumps. Add *sugar* and/or *salt* as desired and cook till the cereal butter thickens and serve hot. Ajja is better eaten fresh. This makes six small servings.

Ajja is a breakfast cereal that may be served at lunch or dinner too. It is especially recommended for new mothers.

CRACKED WHEAT PORRIDGE

QINCH'E

UTENSILS: deep cooking pot (6 to 8 quarts)

INGREDIENTS:
2 cups	cracked wheat
1 cup	butter (spiced)
1 cup	water
2 cups	milk
to taste	salt

PREPARATION: Wash *cracked wheat* in cold running water. Boil *water, milk,* half of the *butter* and *salt* in the cooking pot. Add cracked wheat to boiling water over low heat to prevent burning. Stir gently to keep from sticking. When wheat is soft remove from heat and add the remaining butter. Serve hot. Makes 6 servings. Refrigerate. Warm on low heat for serving.

Qinch'e, like genfo, is a breakfast favorite which is popular with any meal as a side dish.

Butter

SCRAMBLED EGGS

YENQULAL FIRFIR

UTENSILS: medium mixing bowl
frying pan

INGREDIENTS:

2	large eggs
to taste	salt
1 Tbsp.	green pepper chopped
1/2 tbsp.	garlic powder
1/2 tsp.	ginger powder
1/2 tsp.	cardamom
1/2 cup	oil
1/2 cup	onions

PREPARATION: In a medium mixing bowl, mix the *eggs*, *salt*, *green pepper*, *onions*, *cardamom*, *garlic* and *ginger* powder. Add mixture in the hot frying pan with oil. Stir with a fork until cooked. Remove when ready and serve hot.

Yenqulal Firfir is another favorite dish. Easy to prepare and appetizing.

OMELETTE

ENQULAL T'IBS

UTENSILS: medium mixing bowl
frying pan
spatula

INGREDIENTS:

2	large eggs
to taste	salt
1 Tbsp.	green pepper, chopped
1 Tbsp.	onion, finely chopped
1/4 tsp.	garlic powder
1/4 tsp.	ginger powder
1/4 tsp.	cardamom
2 Tbsp.	oil

PREPARATION: In a medium mixing bowl, mix the *eggs*, *salt*, *green pepper*, *onion*, *garlic* and *ginger* powder, and *cardamom*. Add mixture in the hot frying pan and cook for two to three minutes. When ready fold into half and serve hot.

Enqulal T'ibs is similar to Spanish omelette, when served with ginfilfil on the side, it is a full meal by itself.

Soups

CHICKEN SOUP

YEDORO SHORBA

UTENSILS: medium mixing bowl
large cooking pot

INGREDIENTS: 1/2   chicken
4 Tbsp   oil
1/2 cup   onion chopped
1/4 tsp   ginger mashed
1/4 tsp   garlic mashed
15 cups   water
to taste   salt

PREPARATION: Wash *chicken* thoroughly in 3 cups of water. Debone chicken and soak in two cups of water with two slice of lemon.
Cook onion with *oil* over a low heat stirring constantly so that the color does not change and to prevent it from sticking. Add the *garlic* and *ginger* and cook for 4-5 minutes. Add the *chicken* and cook for 6 to 10 minutes more. Add 10 cups of lukewarm *water* and bring to boil for 15 minutes. Serve hot. Makes 4 servings.

Yedoro Shorba is not an everyday soup. It is usually prepared for children & convalescents.

KIDNEY BEAN SOUP

YEADENGWARE SHORBA

UTENSILS: medium mixing bowl
large cooking pan

INGREDIENTS:

1 1/2 cups	kidney beans
1/2 cup	leeks chopped
1/3 cup	carrots peeled
1/3 cup	potatoes peeled & chopped
2 Tbsp	pastini
to taste	salt
3 cups	broth
10 cups	water

PREPARATION: Soak *kidney beans* in 4 cups of *water* overnight. Drain and add 6 cups of water in a large cooking pan. Bring to boil, reduce the heat and simmer for 1 hour. Add the *leek*, *carrots, salt, broth*, and cook for 8 minutes. Add the *potatoes* and *pastini*. Cook for 15 minutes more. Remove from heat and serve hot.

Yeadengware Shorba like most soup is full of nutrition. With pieces of injera or bread added to it, it satisfies the hungry stomach.

LENTIL SOUP

YEMISIR SHORBA

UTENSILS: Medium mixing bowl
large cooking pot

INGREDIENTS:
1 1/2 cups	of lentils
1/2 cup	onion (chopped)
1/4 tsp	ginger (mashed)
1/4 tsp	garlic (mashed)
to taste	salt
10 cups	water

PREPARATION: Wash *lentils* thoroughly in 3 cups of water. Cook onion with oil over a low heat stirring constantly so that the color does not change and to prevent it from sticking. Add the *garlic* and *ginger* and cook for 4 - 5 minutes. Add lentils and cook for 5 minutes more. Add 7 cups of lukewarm *water* and bring to boil for 15 minutes. Serve hot. Serves 4.

Yemisir Shorba is an everyday soup. With pieces of injera or bread added, it is considered very tasty.

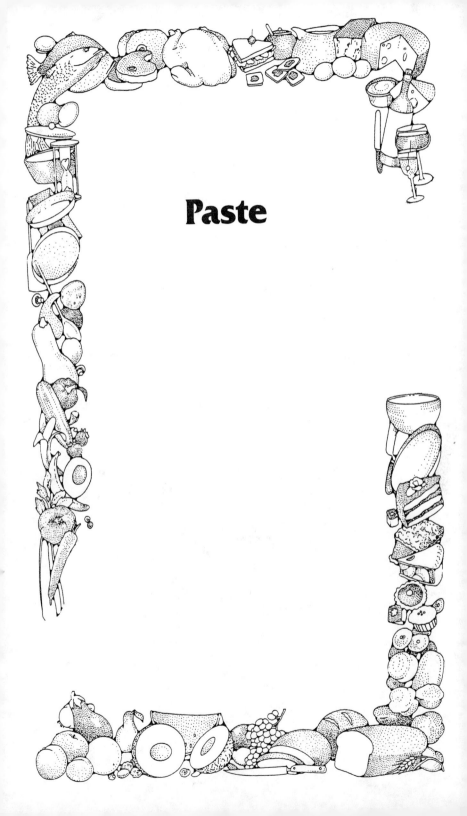

Paste

BARLEY PASTE

YEGEBS SILJO

UTENSILS: medium cooking pot
medium frying pan
medium mixing bowl
air-tight container

INGREDIENTS:

4 cups	barley flour
1 Tbsp.	fenugreek
1/2 cup	mustard powder
2 cups	sunflower juice
1/2 cup	garlic powder
1/2 cup	ginger powder
1/4 cup	lemon juice
2-3 cups	water
to taste	salt

PREPARATION: *Barley Powder*—Soak barley seeds in water for about 1 hour. Drain the water and spread on a clean cloth to dry for 2 to 3 hours in the sun. Roast lightly, grind into a fine powder and set aside.

Roast *fenugreek* over low heat. Grind to a fine powder and set aside.

Boil *barley flour* and *fenugreek* in 4 cups water until it thickens. Put into a bowl and allow to cool. Pour 1 cup cold water on top but do not mix. When cold, slowly pour off the water. Rubbing by hand, add *mustard, garlic*, and *ginger* powders. Add *sunflower juice* until mixture thickens. Add *lemon juice* and mix well. Pour into an air-tight container and let stand for three days before consumption. Store in refrigerator. Yields 6-8 servings.

Yegebs Siljo is a popular dish during fasting. May be eaten with injera or bread. It is a vegetarian dish.

Barley

BROAD BEAN PASTE

YEBAQELA SILJO

UTENSILS: medium pan
medium frying pan
medium mixing bowl
mortar and pestle (for pounding)
blender

INGREDIENTS:

4 cups	bean powder
2 cups	sunflower water
1/2 cup	garlic (fresh)
1/2 cup	ginger (fresh)
1/2 cup	mustard powder
2-3 sprigs	rue (fresh)
to taste	salt
4-8 cups	water

PREPARATION: *Bean Powder*—Soak 6 cups of *beans* overnight. Drain water and spread out beans on a tray to dry. Roast the dried beans over low heat in medium frying pan for 10-15 minutes. Cool and pound beans gently and remove pods by winnowing. Wash in cold running water and leave until completely dry on a tray. Grind into a fine powder.

Boil sunflower seeds in medium heat in 3 cups of water for 25-30 minutes. Remove from heat and drain off liquid. Pound sunflower seeds until it becomes like paste. Add 4 cups cold water into paste and strain. Discard the paste and put *sunflower water* in a bowl.

Boil 4 cups of *water*. Add *bean powder* slowly, stirring. Add *salt*. Cook over low heat for 20-25 minutes and remove from heat. Put mixture in a bowl and add 2 cups cold water. Let sit until cool. When cool pour off water and add sunflower water and mix by hand or mixer. Stick peeled *garlic* with tooth picks and add into the mixture. Grind *ginger*, wrap in clean gauze with *rue* and add to mixture. Add *mustard powder* and mix to form a paste. Cover tightly and leave for 7 days. Serve cold. May be stored indefinitely in refrigerator. Serves about 6.

Yebaqela Siljo is a popular dish during fasting. May be eaten with bread or injera. It is a vegetarian dish.

Paste

CHICK PEA DIP

HUMUS

UTENSILS: blender
medium mixing bowls
spatula

INGREDIENTS:

2 cans (15 oz. each)	chick peas
1/3 cup	fresh lemon juice
1/2 cup	sesame oil
3 cloves	garlic (crushed)
a snip	fresh mint
to taste	salt
2 Tbsp.	olive oil

PREPARATION: Drain liquid from *chick peas*. Reserve 1/4 cup liquid. Place chick peas, *lemon juice*, and 1/4 cup of the reserved liquid in a blender container and cover. Puree, scraping sides of container frequently with spatula until smooth. Transfer chick-pea mixture to medium sized bowl. Add *sesame oil, garlic*, snipped *mint* and *salt* and stir well. Cover and refrigerate for at least six hours. Taste and adjust seasonings. Pour chick-pea mixture into dip bowl forming well in center. Pour *olive oil* into well. Serve at room temperature garnished with mint leaves and olives. Eat with pita bread or crackers. Serves 6 to 8.

Humus is a tasty dish. Served on occasions.

FLAX PASTE

YETELBA LIQUT'

UTENSILS: medium cooking pan
medium size mixing bowl
mortar and pestle

INGREDIENTS: 1 cup   flax seeds
1/2 cup   water

PREPARATION: Roast *flax seeds* in a pan over low heat, until golden brown, for 10 minutes. Remove from heat and let cool. When cool pound with mortar and pestle into fine powder. Add *water* to the powder and mix into paste making sure it does not turn to liquid. Serve paste with bread or injera. Store unused powder or refrigerate paste in jar. Serves 4-6.

Yetelba Liqut' makes a light snack and a fast meal. Replaces butter on toast for breakfast during Lent.

Flax

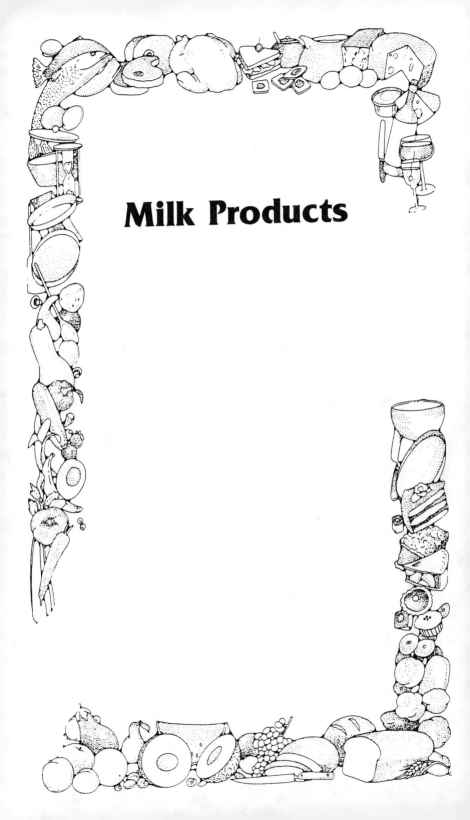

Milk Products

Exotic Ethiopian Cooking

COTTAGE CHEESE

AYIB

UTENSILS: medium mixing bowl with cover
large cooking pot
sieve

INGREDIENTS: 1/2 gallon   sour milk

PREPARATION: In a clean container pour *sour milk,* cover and shake until butter separates from the milk. Remove the butter and pour the Aryera* into a large cooking pot. Cook the Aryera over a low heat until cheese forms on top. Allow the Aryera and Aggwat** to cool. Strain through a sieve to remove the cheese. Store in a covered container and refrigerate. Use as needed.

Ayib is what cottage cheese is to the west. It is usually served with chicken we't, siga we't or mixed with collard greens, or red pepper.

* *Aryera (Butter milk)* is the residual or remains after the butter is removed from the sour milk.

** *Aggwat (whey)* is what remains after the cheese is removed from the Areyera.

237

YOGURT

IRGO

UTENSILS: large cooking pot
large mixing bowl with cover

INGREDIENTS: 5 cups   milk
1 piece   fresh rue

PREPARATION: In a large cooking pot boil *milk* for three to five minutes. Pour milk in a large mixing bowl. Add *rue* and cover at room temperature for 3-5 days. Store in a cool place and use as needed.

Irgo is to Ethiopia what yogurt is to the west. It is served with hot and spicy stew as a side order. It minimizes the burning feeling as well as complimenting the hot spicy stew.

Glossary of Basic Terms

Abesha—Abyssinia

Abish—Fenugreek

Abseet—Yeast

Afrinj—Spiced powdered pepper
seeds, condiment

Ajja—Oats

Alich'a—Spiced but mild stew (no
berbere)

Ambasha—Decorated Pan Bread

Annebabero—3 or 4 layers of injera
coated with berbere and spiced
butter

Asharo—Roasted ground grain

Assa—Fish

Ater—Green peas

At'mit—Cream of wheat or oats

Ato—Mr

Awaze—Red pepper paste

Ayib—Cottage cheese

Azifa—Lentils blended with oil, lemon,
green pepper, onions, and spices

Baqela—Broad beans

Berbere—Chili pepper or a condiment
mixture in which chili pepper is
predominant

Besso—Barley meal

Boqollo—Corn

Biqil—Germinated wheat

Birz—Honey mixed with water

Bozena—Pea flour sauce

Bunna—Coffee

But'echa'—Chick pea paste

Che'che'bsa—Crushed pan bread in
spiced butter & red pepper

Chi'kko—Spiced barley meal in butter

Dabbe—Form of bread referred with
chick pea

Dabbo—Bread

Dabbo Qolo—Roasted wheat in the
shape of nuts

Dereq—Dry

Dirqosh—Dried powdered injera

Dinich—Potato

Doro—Chicken

Doyyo—Thick split pea sauce with
meat and bones

Dullet—Spiced tripe, liver and beef

Duqet—Powder

Enqulal—egg

Fitfit—Injera mixed with spiced stew

Gebs—Barley

Genfo—Thick porridge

Ginfilfil—Injerea mixed with spiced
stew

Ginter—Slightly boiled beef

Gesho—Hops

Gomen—Collard green

Gush—Premature T'ella

Hibist—Steamed bread

Hulbet—Fenugreek (Adere language
Harer)

Humus—Dip made from chick pea
powder

Hodiqa—Kidney, liver, intestine are
referred to as "hodiqa"

Infirfir—Pea flour paste

Injera—Pancake like national bread—
Aenjera

Inset—False banana

Irgo—Yogurt

Kefa—A province in South West
Ethiopia

Kik—Split peas

Kitfo—Chopped beef seasoned in
butter and mit'mit'a

LebLeb—Medium rare

LemLem—Slightly rare
Liqut—paste
Mashila—Sorghum
Mar—Honey
Mesob—Decorated dining straw basket
Milas—Tongue
Mereq—Gravy
Misir—Lentils
Mit'mit'a—Very hot chili powder
Mit'in—Spiced peas
Minchet—Finely chopped
Muz—Banana
Nifro—All cereals when boiled
Nit'ir—Purified
Nech'—White
Qarya—Green pepper
Qibe—Butter
Qoch'o—Dish made from false banana stem
Qitta—Crackers
Qwant'a—Strips of dried meat
Ruz—Rice
Salayish—Shredded beef stew
Samma—Nettle, stingy leaves
Sambossa—Pastry filled with boiled lentils
Sember—Tripe
Siksikosh—Beef stew with ribs
Sinde—Wheat
Senafich'—Ethiopian mustard
Shimbra—Chick pea

Shiro—Powdered legumes carefully blended with spices and red pepper
Siga—Meat
Siljo—Mustard or Paste
Sinnig—When fresh green pepper is stuffed with onion
Suff—Sunflower seeds
T'ej—Beverage brewed from honey and hops
T'ella—Beverage brewed from barley, finger millet, and hops
Telba—Flax seeds
T'ift'ire—Cotton seeds
T'ihlo—Barley balls
T'ef—Rye like grain, indigenous to Ethiopia
Tringo—Citron fruit (cédrat)
T'iqur—Black
T'ire—Raw
Teemateem—Tomatoes
Wat'ela—Spiced beef jerky
Weiyzerit—Miss
Weiyzero—Mrs
We't—Spiced stew
Ye—Conjunction "of", usually followed by a noun
Yehil—Extract of cereal (as for oil, etc.)
Yeteqememe—Spiced
Zinjibil—Ginger
Zigni—Ground beef stew

Measures: Tables of Equivalence

OVEN TEMPERATURES

Fahrenheit	Centigrade	General term and gas-regulo setting	
240	115	very slow	(1/4)
290	145	slow	(1)
355	180	moderate	(4)
400	205	moderately hot	(6)
430	220	hot	(7)
470	245	very hot	(9)

WEIGHTS

metric	British/U.S.	metric	British/U.S.
10 g	0.36 oz	500 g (1/2 kg)	1 lb 1.18 oz
14 g	0.5 oz	567 g	1 1/4 lb
28 g	1.0 oz	600 g	1 lb 5.4 oz
42 g	1.5 oz	675 g	1 1/2 lb
50 g	1.8 oz	731 g	1 lb 10.0 oz
56 g	2.0 oz	750 g (3/4 kg)	1 lb 10.7 oz
70 g	2.5 oz	785 g	1 3/4 lb
90 g	3.2 oz	908 g	2 lb
100 g	3.6 oz	1 kg	2 lb 3.7 oz
113 g	4.0 oz (1/4 lb)	1 kg 137 g	2 1/2 lb
126 g	4.5 oz	1 1/2 kg	3 lb 5.4 oz
150 g	5.3 oz	2 kg	4 lb 7.2 oz
169 g	6.0 oz	2 kg 270 g	5 lb
200 g	7.1 oz	3 kg	6 lb 10.8 oz
227 g	8.0 oz (1/2 lb)	3 kg 632 g	8 lb
250 g (1/4 kg)	8.9 oz	5 kg	11 lb 2 oz
300 g	10.7 oz		
340 g	12.0 oz (3/4 lb)		
397 g	14.0 oz		
454 g	16.0 oz (1 lb)		

MEASURES OF CAPACITY (equivalences between fluid ounces* and millilitres, more exact than those used in the recipes)

metric (ml)	British fl oz*	metric (ml)	British fl oz*
5 (1tsp)	0.18	196	7
15 (1 tbs)	0.5	227	8
22.5	0.8	250 (1/4 litre)	8.9
28	1	280	10
30 (2 tbs)	1.1	336	12
42	1.5	392	14
45 (3 tbs)	1.6	454	16
56	2	500 (1/2 litre)	17.9
60 (4 tbs)	2.1	560	20
70	2.5	600	21.4
75	2.7	672	24
84	3	750 (3/4 litre)	26.8
98	3.5	896	32
112	4	1 litre	35.7
125	4.5	1 1/2 litres	53.6
140	5	2 litres	71.4
150	5.4	2 1/2 litres	89.3
168	6	3 litres	107.1

*The British fluid ounce is fractionally smaller than the U.S. one. This difference, which is of the order of 4%, may be disregarded unless you are dealing with very large quantities.

MEASURES OF CAPACITY *(for those still wedded to pints and cups)*

British	American	fl oz	metric (ml)
	1/4 cup	2	57
1/4 cup		2.5	71
	1/3 cup	2.7	76
1/3 cup		3.3	95
	1/2 cup (1/4 pint)	4	113
1/2 cup (1/4 pint)		5	142
	3/4 cup	6	170
3/4 cup		7.5	198
	1 cup (1/2 pint)	8	227
1 cup (1/2 pint)		10	284
	2 cups (1 pint)	16	454
2 cups (1 pint)		20	567
	3 cups	24	680
3 cups		30	850
	4 cups (2 pint)	32	907
4 cups (2 pint)		40	1134

Oil Seeds

English Name	Latin Name	Amharic Name
Cabbage Seed (Rape Seed)	Brassica Napus	Gomen Zer
Cotton Seed	Gossypium sp.	T'ift'ire
Flax Seed (Linseed)	Linum sp.	Telba
Ethiopian mustard Seed	Brassica Carinata	Senafich
Sesame Seed	Sesamum indicum	Seli't
Sunflower Seed	Helianthus amnuus	Suff
NONE	Maesa lanceolata	Qilwa
Niger Seed	Guizetia abyssinica	Nug

Spices

Common English Name	Latin Name	Amharic Name
Anise	Pimpinella Anisum	Insilal
Bishop's Weed (Ajwan)	Trachyspermum ammi	Netch Azmud
Birds eye-chili	Capsicum frutescens	Mit'mita
Black cumin (Love-in-a-mist)	Nigella sativa	Tikur Azmud
Black peppercorns	Piper nigrum	K'undo berbere
Cinnamon	Cinnamomum zeylanicum	K'erefa
Cloves	Eugenia caryophyllata	K'rinfud
Corriander	Coriandrum Sativum	Dimbilal
Cumin	Cuminum cyminum	Kemun
Dill	Anethum Graveolens	Insilal
False cardomom (Grain of paradise)	Aframomum sp.	Kewrerima
Fennel	Foeniculum vulgare	Insilal
Fenugreek	Trigonella foenum graecum	Abish
Garlic	Allium sativum	Netch'Shinkurt
Ginger	Zingiber officianale	Zinjibil
Long pepper	Piper longum	Timiz
Long nutmeg	Myristica sp.	Gewz
Mint	Mentha sp.	Iban or Naana
Mustard seed	Brassica nigra	Senafich
Red pepper (chili)	Capsicum frutescens	Berbere
Red shallots	Allium cepa ssp.	Key Shinkurt
Rue	Ruta graveolens	Tena Adam
Sacred basil	Ocimum sanctum var. anisatum	Besobila
Savory	Satureja sp.	Tosinyi
Turmeric	Curcuma longa	Ird

FOOD COMPOSITION TABLES
FOR USE IN ETHIOPIA

Research project sponsored by
Swedish International Development Authority (SIDA),
Stockholm, Sweden
and
the Ministry of Public Health of Ethiopia.

Analytical data reported in these tables are results of a collaborative project carried out by Gunnar Ärgen Institute of Medical Chemistry University of Uppsala and Rosalind Gibson, the Food Analytical Department Children's Nutrition Unit, Addis Ababa.

CEREALS AND GRAIN PRODUCTS

COMPOSITION IN TERMS OF 100 GRAMS EDIBLE PORTION

Item No	Food and Description	Local Name	Food Energy (Calories)	Moisture (Percent)	Nitrogen (Grams)	Protein (Grams)	Fat (Grams)	Carbo-hydrate (Grams)	Fiber (Grams)	Ash (Grams)	Calcium (Milli grams)	Phos-phorous (Milli grams)	Iron (Milli grams)	B Carotene Equiv. (Micro grams)	Thiamine (Milli grams)	Riboflavin (Milli grams)	Niacin (Milli grams)	Ascorbic Acid (Milli grams)
1	**BARLEY** WHOLE GRN	GEBS	334	11.3	1.7	9.3	1.9	75.4	3.7	2	47	325	10.2	TRACE	0.32	0.12	6.3	—
	GERMINATED	"	183	51.6	0.9	4.9	1.2	41.1	3.4	1.1	23	130	5.1	—	0.15	—	2.5	3
	FLOUR	"	344	9.2	2.0	10.8	2.4	74.3	3.7	2.3	73	438	15.9	0	0.08	0.15	6.6	0
	ROASTED	"	359	4.2	1.5	9.0	1.9	82.3	3.4	2.1	52	380	19.5	0	0.23	0.15	3.8	0
	SPLIT	"	334	11.3	1.4	7.9	1.4	78.0	1.8	1.5	45	299	8.9	0		0.04	5.5	0
2	**CORN, MAIZE** WHOLE	BOQOLLO	356	12.4	1.4	8.3	4.6	73.4	2.2	1.3	6	276	4.2	0	0.38	0.09	2.1	2
	WHITE VARIETY	"	363	10.7	1.5	8.6	4.6	74.9	2.6	1.3		282	4.4		0.22	0.08	3.9	
	YELLOW VARIETY	"	363	10.7	1.5	8.5	4.7	74.7	3.2	1.4		301	5.3		0.10	0.06	5.4	
	GERMINATED	"	319	19.0	1.5	8.8	2.7	68.9	3.3	1.1	38	210	3.5	0			3.0	4
	TOASTED		380	6.7	1.4	8.7	4.6	78.7	2.4	1.6	7	291	4.3		0.13	0.06	2.3	4
	SPLIT		362	11.7	1.6	8.1	5.1	73.8	2.6	1.3	3	285	3.5	TRACE	0.36	0.12	2.2	2
	FRESH ON COB		349	14.1	1.6	8.8	4.3	71.4	2.7	1.3	2	303	3.1	TRACE	0.33	0.10	2.1	1
	FLOUR FROM MATURE GRAIN	NEFRO	366	10.1	1.5	8.3	4.7	75.9	2.1	1.4	9	267	10.3	TRACE	0.30	0.11	1.9	2
	COOKED MAIZE		231	42.4	1.1	5.9	2.6	47.9	1.8	1.3	14	222	2.9		0.19	0.05	0.2	—
3	**EMMER WHEAT** WHOLE GRAIN	AJJA	336	11.0	2.3	12.4	2.3	72.2	2.4	1.9	55	341	8.8	0	0.41	0.13	7.1	2
	SPLIT GRAIN	" / SINDE	339	10.5	2.6	14.4	2	71.8	1.7	1.6	40	380	8.8	0	0.34	0.12	5.4	8
4	**WHEAT** WHOLE GRAIN WHITE	SINDE	339	10.8	1.8	10.3	1.9	71.9	3	1.5	49	276	7.5	0	0.34	0.09	2.9	4
	BLACK		336	11.3	1.9	10.4	1.9	74.6	3	1.8	52	319	12.9	TRACE	0.27	0.12	3.4	
	GERMINATED WHEAT WHOLE GRN ROAST.		343	9.4	2.3	13.2	1.9	73.9	3.3	1.7	0.49	310	11.6	0			4.7	13
	FLOUR	QOLLO	369	3.1	1.6	8.9	2.3	86.2	3.9	1.9	49	362	15.7	0	0.10	0.07	4.3	
	FLOUR	DUQET	323	12.7	1.9	10.5	1.4	74.2	1.6	1.3	46	158	4.1		0.42	0.11	3.1	
5	**MILLET** WHOLE GRAIN	DAGUSSA	326	12.1	1.3	7.2	1.4	77.1	5.6	3.3	386	220	85.1	0	0.20	0.09	0.8	1
6	**SORGHUM** WHOLE GRAIN WHITE	MASHILLA ZENGADA	338	12.1	1.3	7.1	2.8	76.5	2.3	1.6	30	282	7.8	0	0.54	0.12	3.3	3
	RED	MASHILLA NEFRO	338	12.4	1.3	7.1	3.1	75.8	3.7	1.7	35	258	9.6	TRACE	0.29	0.12	3.4	4
	COOKED	NEFRO	100	72.5	0.4	2.2	0.8	23.6	0.7	1	12	95	8.0			0.04	1.6	0
7	**T'EF** WHITE	NECH T'EF	339	10.4	1.9	11.1	2.4	73.6	3	2.5	156	366	18.9	0	0.64	0.14	1.8	1
	RED	KEY T'EF	336	11.1	1.8	10.5	2.7	73.1	3.5	3.1	157	348	58.9	TRACE	0.32	0.13	1.7	1
	T'EF FLOUR WHITE		338	10.9	1.6	9.3	2.4	74.9	2	2.4	130	354	23.4	0	0.42	0.10	1.8	2
	RED		335	10.8	1.7	9.6	2.7	73.8	2.7	2.9	150	363	50	TRACE	0.07	0.14	1.2	1

ANALYSIS PER 100 GRAMS OF THE PRODUCT

STARCHY ROOTS, TUBERS AND FRUITS

COMPOSITION IN TERMS OF 100 GRAMS EDIBLE PORTION

Item No	Food and Description	Local Name	Food Energy Calories	Moisture Percent	Nitrogen Grams	Protein Grams	Fat Grams	Carbo-hydrate Grams	Fiber Grams	Ash Grams	Calcium Milli grams	Phos-phorous Milli grams	Iron Milli grams	B Carotene Micro grams	Thiamine Milli grams	Riboflavin Milli grams	Niacin Milli grams	Ascorbic Acid Milli grams
1	FALSE BANANA STEM PITH GREY & WHITE	INSET QOCH'O BULLA	200	48.7	0.2	0.6	0.3	49.0	1.2	0.9	82	36	3.7	0	0.03	0.04	0.3	0
	FERMENTED FLOUR	"	186	53.5	0.2	0.5	0.4	44.8	2.1	0.8	70	45	7.9	TRACE	0.04	0.05	0.2	0
	BAKED		196	49.7	0.3	0.9	0.2	47.7	1.2	1.6	77	60	10.1	0		.10	0.2	1
			198	48.4	0.2	1.0	0.2	48.0	1.8	1.7	83	43	2.4	0				0
2	"BANANA, COMMON MUSA" RIPE	MUZ	79	77.7	0.2	0.8	0.6	19.9	0.4	1.1	8	30	0.5	0	0.04	.10	1.0	2
	POTATO RAW	DINICH	87	78.1	0.3	1.3	0.1	20.4	1.4	1.1	14	57	2.3	0	0.08	0.03	1	14
4	SWEET POTATO RAW	SUKAR DINICH	126	67.4	0.3	1.3	0.2	30.0	1.1	1.1	52	34	3.4	0	0.08	0.05	0.9	9
5	YAM	ANCHOTE	9.5	74.5	.7	3.1	.1	21.2	1.7	1.1	119		1.8					

ANALYSIS PER 100 GRAMS OF THE PRODUCT

GRAIN LEGUMES AND LEGUME PRODUCT
COMPOSITION IN TERMS OF 100 GRAMS EDIBLE PORTION

Item No	Food and Description	Local Name	Food Energy Calories	Moisture Percent	Nitrogen Grams	Protein Grams	Fat Grams	Carbo-hydrate Grams	Fiber Grams	Ash Grams	Calcium Milli grams	Phos-phorous Milli grams	Iron Milli grams	B Carotene Micro grams	Thiamine Milli grams	Riboflavin Milli grams	Niacin Milli grams	Ascorbic Acid Milli grams
1	**BROAD BEANS** WHOLE SEED	BAQELA	344	11	4.0	21.5	1.4	63.2	9.6	2.9	99	420	8.4	TRACE	.44	0.30	2.1	2
	WHOLE SEED FRESH IN POD	NEFRO	149	61.1	1.7	9.9	0.6	27.6	7.5	1.5	63	189	2.1	TRACE	0.17	0.23	2.9	7
	COOKED		144	62.0	1.9	9.9	0.7	26.5	3.7	1.5	54	165	2.9	TRACE		0.20	1.0	0
	SPLIT		343	10.6	4.7	24.8	1.5	60.1	1.9	3.0	47	469	14.5	TRACE	0.72	0.40	1.9	3
2	**CHICK PEA** WHOLE SEED	SHIMBRA	363	10.5	3.2	17.4	5.2	63.9	9.4	3.2	251	231	14.3	TRACE	0.43	0.12	1.5	3
	FRESH		102	77.6	0.9	4.6	1.0	19.1	4.2	0.8	52	73	6.3	TRACE	0.18	0.09	3.8	93
	TOASTED		383	5.8	3.2	17.5	5.3	68.3	8.7	3.1	238	291	11.0		0.08	0.14	2.0	
	SPLIT		368	10.0	3.3	17.6	6.0	64.4	2.7	3.1	96	216	11.6	TRACE	0.69	0.16	1.2	4
	FLOUR		372	8.0	3.6	19.4	5.8	63.0	4.8	3.4	117	330	68.2	2411	0.32	0.11	0.9	
3	**FENUGREEK** WHOLE SEED	ABISH	381	8.7	4.3	21.7	8.2	58.3	9.8	3.2	178	296	34.1	TRACE	0.32	0.43	1.7	3
4	**KIDNEY BEAN** WHOLE SEED	ADENGWARE	346	9.5	3.7	19.1	1.6	65.4	6.7	3.9	144	414	8.7	TRACE	0.43	0.14	2.0	0
5	**LENTIL** WHOLE SEED	MISIR	344	10.2	4.0	22.6	1.0	63.2	4.8	3.0	68	359	28.3	TRACE	0.37	0.15	1.6	3
	SPLIT		350	9.8	4.2	23.5	1.1	63.7	2.4	2.8	36	317	43.1	TRACE	0.29	0.14	1.8	
6	**PEAS** FLOUR	SHIRO	345	10.7	3.7	20.1	1.4	64.8	4.3	3.0	79	309	13.9	TRACE	0.30	0.16	2.4	3
	SPLIT		347	10.5	4.0	21.6	1.4	63.3	2.8	2.8	64	347	13.6	TRACE	0.51	0.13	2.7	4
7	**PEANUT** DRIED SHELLED	OCHOLONI	545	5.7	4.4	23.0	42.5	26.8	3.5	2.0	51	252	3.0	0			31.2	0
	PEANUT CAKE		349	7.7	7.8	40.8	4.7	41.2	7.6	5.6	131	600	79.4	0				
8	**SOYA BEAN** FULL FAT SOY FLOUR		420	6.8	6.3	34.7	18.6	37.1	5.1	4.8	200		13.8		1.06			
	"SOY FLOUR, DEFATTED"			8.0	8.9	50.0												

ANALYSIS PER 100 GRAMS OF THE PRODUCT

NUTS AND SEEDS
COMPOSITION IN TERMS OF 100 GRAMS EDIBLE PORTION

Item No	Food and Description	Local Name	Food Energy (Calories)	Moisture (Percent)	Nitrogen (Grams)	Protein (Grams)	Fat (Grams)	Carbohydrate (Grams)	Fiber (Grams)	Ash (Grams)	Calcium (Milli grams)	Phosphorous (Milli grams)	Iron (Milli grams)	B Carotene Equiv (Micro grams)	Thiamine (Milli grams)	Riboflavin (Milli grams)	Niacin (Milli grams)	Ascorbic Acid (Milli grams)
1	COTTON SEEDS SEED	T'IFT'IRE		9.8	8.7	45.1				6.8	210	1254	9.4				508	0
2	"LIN SEED" FAX SEED WHOLE SEED PRESS CAKE OIL CAKE	TELBA	490 354	5.8 9.9	3.2 3.7	17.0 19.3	29.7 3.9	43.9 62.1	10.3 9.5	3.6 4.8	227 309	454 528	29.4 58.8	0 0	0.35	0.11 0.21	2.0 2.0 3.6	1
3	NIGER SEED WHOLE SEED FLOUR EXTRACTED PRESS CAKE	NUG	486 309 346	5.9 11.3 7.6	3.3 4.9 4.4	18.3 26.7 23.9	33.4 4.4 5.8	37.8 44.2 52.4	18.3 18.9 24.0	5.9 10.5 8.0	331 615 578	843 1581 1307	72.5 84.3 212.2	0 0 0	0.88	0.43	4.1	0
4	KALE SEEDS	GOMEN ZER	483	6.1	3.9	24.5	35.0	26.1	7.8	8.3	368	594	392.0	650	0.54	0.32	7.0	0
5	PUMPKIN SEED WHOLE SEED	YEDUBA FERE	501	7.1	4.0	30.0	37.4	27.1	22.7	3.8	74	841	21.7	TRACE	0.29	0.12	4.9	
6	SAFFLOWER WHOLE SEED FAT EXTRACTED CRUSHED	SUFF	474 369 489	5.3 5.7 6.3	2.3 3.4 2.2	11.3 16.5 10.5	24.3 1.0 28.7	57.3 74.6 52.2	30.3 44.3 27.6	2.1 2.2 2.4	162 189 145	309 310 460	11.8 14.0 6.9	0 0 0	0.44	0.08 .15	1.3 0.8 1.1	
7	SESAME WHOLE SEED WHITE BLACK	SELIT	582 565	5.8 5.5	3.2 3.7	16.7 19.3	53.7 50.6	18.2 18.4	25.2 12.9	5.6 6.2	1017 1483	732 578	56.2		0.22 0.14	0.02 0.05	7.3 8.7	
8	SUNFLOWER WHOLE SEED OIL CAKE PROTEIN CONCENTRATE		488	5.5 8.5	2.7 7.7	13.5 44.5	29.6 2.5	47.4		4.0	190	553	50.0		1.16	0.14	3.6 9.5	

ANALYSIS PER 100 GRAMS OF THE PRODUCT

VEGETABLES AND VEGETABLE PRODUCTS
COMPOSITION IN TERMS OF 100 GRAMS EDIBLE PORTION

Item No	Food and Description	Local Name	Food Energy Calories	Moisture Percent	Nitrogen Grams	Protein Grams	Fat Grams	Carbo-hydrate Grams	Fiber Grams	Ash Grams	Calcium Milli grams	Phos-phorous Milli grams	Iron Milli grams	B Carotene Equiv Micro grams	Thiamine Milli grams	Riboflavin Milli grams	Niacin Milli grams	Ascorbic Acid Milli grams
1	CARROT ROOT, RAW	KARROT	42	89.1	0.4	1.7	0.4	7.6	1.0	0.9	31	33	1.3	4780	0.04	0.03	0.5	3
2	ETHIOPIAN KALE LEAVES RAW	GOMEN	37	87.6	0.7	2.8	0.8	6.5	1.5	1.9	260	64	4.1	2330	0.12	0.23	1.2	20
3	GARLIC BULBS RAW	NETCH SHINKURT	118	64.4	0.6	4.1	0.3	29.5	1.1	1.4	36	133	2.1	0	0.21	0.07	0.3	0.3
4	LEEK FRESH, RAW		60	85.3	0.3	1.2	0.6	14.6	1.6	0.8	60	41	1.5	TRACE	0.06	0.06	.6	5
5	OKRA FRUITS, RAW	BAMYA		87.6	0.4	2.3	0.5	8.6	4.5	1.1	79	74	3.8	TRACE	0.06	0.10	0.7	2
6	ONION BULB, RAW, RED	SHINKURT	57	83.8	0.3	1.5	0.4	13.9	0.9	0.7	38	47	1.9	TRACE	0.04	0.06	0.8	2
	ONION SPRING		41	88.5	0.3	1.7	0.6	9.2	1.5	1.0	11	58	2.4	TRACE	0.05	0.06	1.0	9
7	PEPPERS SWEET GREEN		40	88.1	0.3	1.7	0.5	8.7	3.4	0.9	15	38	1.5	500	0.07	0.06	1.0	100
8	PUMPKIN FRUIT RAW	DUBBA	37	88.8	0.2	1.2	0.2	8.9	1.8	0.9	22	41	1.8	280	0.04	0.04	0.7	4
9	TOMATO WHOLE, RAW	TEEMAT-EEM	28	92.5	0.2	1.3	0.7	4.5	1.5	0.7	9	29	0.9	620	0.06	0.05	0.5	9

ANALYSIS PER 100 GRAMS OF THE PRODUCT

FRUITS

COMPOSITION IN TERMS OF 100 GRAMS EDIBLE PORTION

Item No	Food and Description	Local Name	Food Energy Calories	Moisture Percent	Nitrogen Grams	Protein Grams	Fat Grams	Carbo-hydrate Grams	Fiber Grams	Ash Grams	Calcium Milli grams	Phos-phorous Milli grams	Iron Milli grams	B Carotene Micro grams	Thiamine Milli grams	Riboflavin Milli grams	Niacin Milli grams	Ascorbic Acid Milli grams
1	DATE SEED WITHOUT SEED COAT	TEMER	264	28.3	0.6	4.0	3.7	61.0	17.5	3.0	193	133	3.2		0.28	.01	0.1	
2	GRAPE FRUIT FRUIT PULP		37	88.4	0.1	0.6	1.1	9.4	0.7	0.5	31	39	2.4	0	0.07	0.05	0.5	32
3	GUAVA FRUIT, WHOLE, RAW	ZEYETON	60	84.2	0.2	1.1	1.1	13.4	8.7	0.6	17	27	1.6	960	0.02	0.08	0.9	33
4	APPLE YELLOW SMALL BERRIES			76.6			6.0			1.3	46	28	1.4		0.04	0.04	1.3	117
5	LEMONS, CITRUS FRUIT RAW	LOMI	42	88.3	0.1	0.6	2.2	7.8	1.1	0.5	44	24	0.8	TRACE	0.07	0.04	0.7	26
6	ORANGE VERY SMALL FRUIT	BIRTUKAN	38	87.9	0.2	0.7	1.1	9.8	1.4	0.5	50	23	0.8	335	0.08	0.05	0.6	38
7	PRICKLY PEAR RAW	KULQAL		86.4	.1	.8								TRACE	.01	.03	.7	21
8	SUGAR CANE STEM	SHENKORA GEDA	86	76.2	0.1	0.5	0.5	22.2	4.8	0.6	49	37	0.8	0				

ANALYSIS PER 100 GRAMS OF THE PRODUCT

MEAT, POULTRY & FISH
COMPOSITION IN TERMS OF 100 GRAMS EDIBLE PORTION

Item No	Food and Description	Local Name	Food Energy Calories	Moisture Percent	Nitrogen Grams	Protein Grams	Fat Grams	Carbohydrate Grams	Fiber Grams	Ash Grams	Calcium Milli grams	Phosphorous Milli grams	Iron Milli grams	B Carotene Equiv. Micro grams	Thiamine Milli grams	Riboflavin Milli grams	Niacin Milli grams	Ascorbic Acid Milli grams
1	DRIED MEAT	QWANT'A	363	6.2	12.5	64.2	9.8	7.3	1.3	4.5	42	730	15.2	0			15.8	
	MEAT	SIGA	187	76.8	3.2	16.4	1.3	2.3	.5	1.1	3	190	2.1	0			6.3	
2	CHICKEN WHOLE	DORO	120	75.9	3.1	15.5	.6	4.9	0	.9	101		2.0					
	LIVER		123	71.7	2.9	14.5	3.6	7.3	2.8	1.2	11		31.0					
	HEART		-	77.1	2.5	12.5												
3	FISH BONELESS FILET OF TALAPIA	ASSA	60	80.0	2.8	15.1	2.1	0										

ANALYSIS PER 100 GRAMS OF THE PRODUCT

MILK PRODUCTS AND EGGS
COMPOSITION IN TERMS OF 100 GRAMS EDIBLE PORTION

Item No	Food and Description	Local Name	Food Energy Calories	Moisture Percent	Nitrogen Grams	Protein Grams	Fat Grams	Carbohydrate Grams	Fiber Grams	Ash Grams	Calcium Milli grams	Phosphorous Milli grams	Iron Milli grams	B Carotene Equiv. Micro grams	Thiamine Milli grams	Riboflavin Milli grams	Niacin Milli grams	Ascorbic Acid Milli grams
1	BUTTER FROM COW'S MILK	QIBE	714	17.2	0.2	1.3	81.2	1.3	0.1	0.2	24	206	1.5	0	0.05	0.44	0.2	0
2	CHEESE " "	AYIB	135	73.7	2.4	15.2	6.4	2.9	0.2	1.2	110	193	2.3	0	0.05	0.48	0.3	0
	SOUR	"	119	75.4	2.3	16.1	4.4	5.2	0.4	0.9	109	94	3.2	0	0.04	0.21	0.2	2
3	MILK (COW'S)	WETET	76	87.6	0.6	3.4	5.3	3.8	0.1	0.6	89	84	1.0	0	0.03	0.21	0.1	0
4	BUTTER MILK	ARERA	37	91.5	0.5	3.1	1.4	3.2	0	0.6	95	88	1.0		0.04	0.29	0	2
5	YOGHURT	ERGO	82	86.4	0.6	3.5	6.2	3.2	3.8	0.7	52		0.1					1
6	EGGS (HEN'S)	ENKULAL	88	78.6	3.1	18.4	0.1	2.0	0.4	1.0	0	40	1.0				0.2	
	WHITE		352	52.2	2.4	13.9	31.8	2.6	0.9	1.4	47	360	5.3	1014			0.3	

ANALYSIS PER 100 GRAMS OF THE PRODUCT

SPICES

COMPOSITION IN TERMS OF 100 GRAMS EDIBLE PORTION

Item No	Food and Description	Local Name	Food Energy (Calories)	Moisture (Percent)	Nitrogen (Grams)	Protein (Grams)	Fat (Grams)	Carbohydrate (Grams)	Fiber (Grams)	Ash (Grams)	Calcium (Milli grams)	Phosphorous (Milli grams)	Iron (Milli grams)	B Carotene Equiv (Micro grams)	Thiamine (Milli grams)	Riboflavin (Milli grams)	Niacin (Milli grams)	Ascorbic Acid (Milli grams)
1	SPICED POWDERED SEEDS	AFRINJ	372	5.3		11.8	16.3	44.6	24.5	22.0	272	337	45.2	0	.036	.2	.54	2
2	RED PEPPER RAW	BERBERE	85	78.2	.5	2.0	2.5	16.6	8.5	1.6	19	78	3.7	1720	.10	.42	2.3	88
	DRIED	BERBERE	327	9.5	2.2	8.8	10.9	60.1	29.8	10.7	162	331	65.8	24160	.28	.78	9.7	14
3	MIX OF CHILI & OTHER SPICES	BERBERE	332	6.8	2.2	8.8	14.2	53.8	22.3	15.8	216	368	52.6	31790	.23	.45	4.9	36
4	BIRDS EYE CHILI RAW	MIT'MITA	116	69.4	.6	2.2	1.4	23.3	1.8	1.9	49	127	3.3	50600	.04	.22	1.3	44
5	BISHOPWEED DRIED	NETCH AZMUD	471	9.1		14.0	27.2	42.6	22.1	6.3	276	295	63.2	0	.05	.76	4.8	45
6	BLACK	BLACK AZMUD	550	6.7		18.9	39.7	29.3	11.7	9.5	1134	654	34.9	0	.30	.24	3.2	12
7	BLACK PEPPER	K'UNDO BERBERE	396	5.6	—	12.5	9.4	65.4	15.9	6.5	436	459	44.9	0	0	.42	71	9
8	CARDAMOM	KEWRERIMA	357	8.8	—	10.2	3.3	71.6	21.8	3.9	350	193	24.6	0	0	.13	1.5	1
9	CINNAMON	K'EREFA	364	8.7	—	2.8	2.9	81.7	29.3	6.2	147	241	21.1	0	.02	.11	1.5	4
10	CLOVES	K'RINFUD	388	10.7	—	6.0	13.6	60.5	13.8	1.9	419	38	7.4	0	.02	.25	.1	5
11	CORRIANDER	DIMBILAL	425	14.5	—	12.2	14.1	62.4	4.0	5.4	668	122	19.7	TRACE	.07	.14	0	11
12	CUMIN	KEMUN	444	5.7	—	17.3	2.6	45.2	19.3	5.6	820	437	43.1	TRACE	.21	.24	3.6	8
13	HELL		322	7.2	—	—	2.5	74.8	20.0	8.7	5	490	36.2	0	.42	.37	2.7	7
14	LONG NUTMEG	GEWZ	529	12.4	—	12.8	36.6	49.9	16.9	10.3	398	139	15.9	TRACE	.15	.21	1.2	7
15	LONG PEPPER	TIMIZ	380	11.4	—	24.6	8.3	63.6	9.7	2.1	152	220	3.3	TRACE	.09	.37	1.1	7
16	MUSTARD	SENAFICH	526	9.7	—	11.4	32.8	33.1	15.1	5.6	467	220	13.5	0	0	.26	2.0	3
17	BASIL		355	4.5	—	6.6	7.5	60.5	25.9	12.4	1547	653	46.0	TRACE	.17	.36	4.9	8
18	TURMERIC	IRD	357	8.2	—	8.7	5.2	71.0	4.8	6.8	122	453	34.2	0	.07	.10	1.9	8
19	FENUGREEK	ABISH	402	10.4	—	87.7	8.4	53.9	8.7	2.6	171	304	41.0	0	.03	.33	3.5	14

ANALYSIS PER 100 GRAMS OF THE PRODUCT

PREPARED FOODS
COMPOSITION IN TERMS OF 100 GRAMS EDIBLE PORTION

Item No	Food and Description	Local Name	Food Energy (Calories)	Moisture (Percent)	Nitrogen (Grams)	Protein (Grams)	Fat (Grams)	Carbohydrate (Grams)	Fiber (Grams)	Ash (Grams)	Calcium (Milli grams)	Phosphorous (Milli grams)	Iron (Milli grams)	B-Carotene Equiv (Micro grams)	Thiamine (Milli grams)	Riboflavin (Milli grams)	Niacin (Milli grams)	Ascorbic Acid (Milli grams)
BREAD																		
1	BRD. OF BARLEY	INJERA	150	59.6	1	5.2	0.6	33.5	2.1	1.2	48	115	2.7		0.14	0.06	0.2	
2	BRD. OF CORN	INJERA	174	56.3	0.7	4.2	1.4	37.4	1.4	0.7	17	129	6.8		0.12	0.05	.9	0
3	BRD. OF MILLET	INJERA	139	62.1	0.5	2.5	0.3	33.8	2.5	1.3	92	126	22		0.1	0.04	2.1	0
4	BRD. OF SORGHUM	INJERA	115	65.2	0.6	3	0.5	30.5	4.6	0.7	73	100	11.1		0.12	0.04	3.9	
5	BRD. OF TEF	INJERA	162	59.8	0.7	4.2	0.6	33.9	1.7	1.5	64	129	30.5		0.21	0.07	0.8	
6	"INJERA ON RED TEF, DRIED"	YEINJERA DIROOSH		8.2	1.9	11								0			2	1
7	"TINJERA ON WHITE TEF, DRIED"	YEINJERA DIROOSH	367	9.4	2.2	12.8	1.4	74	2	3.3	347	398	34	0	0.62	0.13	1.7	0
8	BREAD OF WHEAT	AMBASHA	227	41.8	1.4	8	0.8	48.0	1.9	1.5	35	219	12.7	0	0.35	0.13	2.6	0
9	BREAD OF 2/3 WHEAT + 1/3 CORN	DABBO	231	41.1	0.6	3.4	2.5	51.4	2.1	1.6	36	90	27					
II	**PORRIDGE**																	
1	CORN	GENFO	138	67.5	0.6	3.3	3.5	24.7	2.1	1	12		2.2	0	0.07	0.02	0.2	
	TEF	GENFO	146	66.9	0.8	4.3	3.3	24.2	1.1	1.4	66		12.6		0.02	0.03	0.3	
III	**SAUCES, SPICED:**																	
1	BROAD BEANS	BAQELA KIK WET	130	69.1	1.1	5.6	5.2	16.4	1.4	3.7	44	40	3	0	0.24	0.23	2.4	1
2	KALE	GOMEN WET	57	88	0.8	3.1	5.7	3.3	1.7	2.4	157		6.5	2700	0.05	0.04	0.5	
3	"LENTIL SPLIT," SAUCE W/BERBERE	MISSIR KIK WET	104	75.7	0.7	3.6	4.6	13.9	0.9	2.6	18	61	7.2	TRACE	0.09	0.04	0.5	0
4	"PEA, SPLIT"	YATER KIKK WET	129	72.7	0.9	4.4	6.7	15.8	1	2.9	21	75	3.7	TRACE	0.16	0.05	0.7	0
5	PEA FLOUR	SHIRO WET	51	86.1	0.4	2.2	1.7	7.1	0.8	2.9	19	33	20.1	TRACE	0.06	0.03	0.4	0
6	MEAT	SIGA WET	206	58.8	2.3	11.8	17.2	9.9	1.5	2.8	33		4					
	"MIXED W/BREAD"	INJERA FITFIT	109	75.4	0.1	0.7	4.6	18.1	1.6	1.3	28	54	4.6					
IV	**SAUCES, UNSPICED:**																	
1	KALE	GOMEN ALICHA	85	83.2	0.5	1.9	7.6	4.9	1.1	2.4	140	25	2.6	1880	0.04	0.11	0.1	0
2	"LENTIL SPLIT, SAUCE W/O BERBERRE"	MISSIR KIK ALICHA	106	76.1	0.7	3.5	4.2	14.5	0.4	1.7	10	50	2.1	0	0.01	0.01	0.3	0
3	"LENTIL, SPLIT"	MISSIR KIK ALICHA	86	76.4	0.9	4.3	1.3	14.6	0.6	3.4	21		4.5	0	0.08	0.04	0.4	0
4	"PEA, SPLIT"	YATER KIK ALICHA	98	73.2	0.9	4.6	1.8	16.5	1.3	3.9	24	47	4.2	0	0.21	0.05	0.8	0
5	PEA FLOUR	SHIRO ALICHA	43	88.5	0.3	1.9	1.4	6.6	.6	2.0	16	83	14.3	TRACE	0.06	0.02	.03	
V	**MISCELLANEOUS**																	
	"COFFEE BEANS," COFFEE LEABCA	BUNNA	96	73.3	0.4	2.4	1.9	20.9	8.2	1.5	32	30	2.3	TRACE	0.15	0.02	1.1	0
2	"CORN + BARLEY, MIX"		305	8.2	1.5	9.2	5.4	66.4	17.3	10.9	1999	170	71.8	2360	0.16	1.61	5.3	25
3			361	12.2	1.5	8.6	3.2	73.3	5.3	2.7	31	330	73.1	0		0.4	5.4	24
4	HONEY WINE	TEJ	8	97.2	0.1	0.3	0.3	1.1	0	0.1	8		0.5			0.05	0.1	
5	LOCAL BEER	TELLA		98.3	0	0.3		0	0								0.2	
6	OIL FOR GOMEN WOT		880	0.5		0	99.5		0									0
7	OIL FROM NIGER SEED		834	0.5		0	99.6		0									1
VI	**OTHERS**																	
1	FENUGREEK LIQUID 1ST EXTRACT		20	97.7	.1	.3	.6	2.5		.3	13	11	19.1	0	0	.04	.2	0
2	2ND EXTRACT		12	96.9	.1	.4	.3	2.1		.3	3	8	2.8			.09	.3	1
VII																		
1	WRUEL	WRUEL	51	85.9	.3	1.5	.6	10.6	.7	1.5	19	30	1.9		.05	.02	.3	0
2	EMMERWHEAT		57	83.7	.5	2.4	.8	11.1	.4	2.1	38	75	3.3			.06	1.7	0

ANALYSIS PER 100 GRAMS OF THE PRODUCT

1. Meat cooked in spice & red pepper
2. Mild chicken stew
3. Fried beef stew
4. Steak Tartar
5. Cottage cheese
6. Injera in sauce mixed over low fire
7. Whole wheat bread
8. Bread made from corn (rolled)
9. Pea flour dissolved in water & mixed with injera
10. Sliced tomatoes & green pepper
11. Sambossa Pastry
12. Potato with green pepper
13. Potato stew
14. Mild split pea sauce
15. Pureed green lentils harmoniously blended with spice
16. Collard green with meat
17. Hot pea flour sauce
18. Fresh tomatoes and green pepper

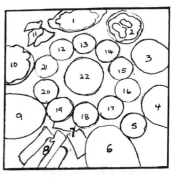

19. Vegetable stew
20. Green pepper paste
21. Vegetable stew (cabbage)
22. Chicken stew

1. Chick pea paste
2. Pureed green lentils harmoniously blended with spices
3. Red pepper (Serrano)
4. White slightly spiced powdered peas
5. Split pea
6. Mild split pea sauce
7. Red pepper (berbere)
8. Chick pea
9. Mild pea flour sauce
10. Garlic
11. Red onion
12. Lentils
13. Hot pea flour sauce

1. Green pepper
2. Red onions
3. Garlic
4. Lime
5. Garlic powder
6. Spiced red pepper (berbere)
7. Basil
8. Chick pea
9. Spiced pea flower
10. Sunflower seeds
11. Cardomom
12. Cardomom seeds

13. Split pea powder
14. Turmeric
15. Bishop's Weed (Ajwan)
16. Mustard seeds
17. Coriander
18. Split pea
19. Cinnamon bark
20. Cinnamon powder
21. Cloves
22. Garlic
23. Birds eye-Chili
24. Corn
25. Black cumin
26. Cardomom pods
27. Cardomom pods
28. Wheat
29. Hops
30. Dill
31. Nutmeg whole
32. Sesame seeds
33. Chili seeds
34. Anise
35. T'eff (red)
36. Split lentils
37. Gum Arabica
38. Emmer wheat

Index

257

RESTAURANTS NAMES
IN
THE USA & CANADA

1. The Blue Nile Restaurant
   2525 Telegraph Avenue
   Berkeley, CA 94704
   (415) 540-6777

2. Blue Nile Restaurant
   317 Braun Ct
   Ann Arbor, MI 48104
   (313) 663-3116

3. Blue Nile Restaurant
   508 Monroe St Greek Town
   Detroit, MI 48226
   (313) 964-6699

4. Blue Nile Restaurant
   103 W. 77th St
   at Columbus Ave
   NY City 10024
   (212) 580-3232

5. Fasika's Ethiopian Cuisine
   2447 18th St NW
   Washington, DC
   (202) 797-7673

6. Kestedamena Restaurant
   5779 W. Venice Blvd
   Los Angeles, CA 90019
   (213) 933-6522

7. Kokeb Restaurant
   926 12th Ave
   Seattle, WA 98122
   (206) 322-0485

8. Meskerem Restaurant
   2434 18th St NW
   Washington, DC
   (202) 462-4100

9. Nyala Restaurant
   39 Grove St
   San Francisco, CA
   (415) 861-0788

10. Queen of Sheba
    5778 Rodeo Rd
    Los Angeles, CA
    (213) 296-1070

11. Rasselas Restaurant
    2801 California St
    San Francisco, CA
    (415) 567-5010

12. Red Sea Ethiopian Cuisine
    2463 18th St NW
    Washington, DC
    (202) 483-5000

13. Rosalinds Restaurant
    1044 S. Fairfax Ave
    Los Angeles, CA 90019
    (213) 936-2486

14. Sheba Restaurant
    1198 Bloor St
    Toronto, Ontario M6H 1N2
    (416) 536-4162

15. Sheba Restaurant
    905 First Ave
    New York, NY 10022
    (212) 752-7222

16. Wanza Restaurant
    6409 Roosevelt Way NE
    Seattle, WA 98115
    (206) 525-3950

17. Zed's Ethiopian Cuisine
    3318 M Street NW
    Washington, DC 20007
    (202) 333-4710

NAMES OF STORES
FOR
SPICES & BASIC INGREDIENTS

*1. Acropolis Food Inc.
1206 Underwood St NW
Washington, DC 20012
(202) 823-1414

**2. Aenjera Bakery
4554 Eisenhower Ave
Alexandria, VA 22304
(703) 823-9356

3. Bombay Bazar
1034 University Ave
Berkeley, CA 94709
(415) 649-0570

4. Bombay Bazar
548 Valencia St
San Francisco, CA
(415) 621-1717

*5. C & K Importing
2791 W. Pico Blvd
Los Angeles, CA 90006
(213) 737-2970   737-2880

6. Ethiopian Wine Company
1631 Kalorama Rd NW
Washington, DC 20009
(202) 326-7403

7. House of Spices
107 O'Leary Drive
Bensenville, IL 60106
(312) 595-2929

8. House of Spices
7908 Fermham Lane
Forestville, MD 20747
(301) 420-1088

9. House of Spices
1086 Maple Ave
Cherryhill, NJ 08002
(609) 665-3292

10. House of Spices
76-17 Broadway
Jackson Heights, NY 11373
(718) 476-1577

11. House of Spices
4101 Walnut St
Philadelphia, PA 19140
(215) 222-1111

12. House of Spices
Keystone Park Shopping Center
13777 N. Centralia Expressway
Dallas, TX 75243
(214) 783-7544

13. House of Spices
5600 Hartsdale
Houston, TX 77036
(713) 266-5224

14. Indian Spices & Appliances
3901 Wilson Blvd
Arlington, VA 22203
(703) 522-0149   522-5232

***15. Maskal Injera
1318 Willow
Caldwell, ID 83605
(208) 454-3300

*16. NTS Enterprises
Import & Wholesales
1170 19th St
Oakland, CA 94607
Telex 3727438 Buscorp
(415) 763-8971

17. Spice House
2343 Birch St
Palo Alto, CA 94306
(415) 326-8811

18. Tu Tu Market
3811A S George Mason Dr
Falls Church, VA 22041
(703) 998-5322

*carries a wide variety of Ethiopian Spices, Beer, Wine and Artcrafts.
**Ready made injera sold at 7-Eleven stores in the Washington Metropolitan area call for your nearest store
***T'ef flour

ETHIOPIAN COOKBOOK ENTERPRISES

3800 POWELL LANE, Suite 404
FALLS CHURCH, VA 22041

Please send _____ copies of Exotic Ethiopian Cooking at
$14.99 plus $2.00 per copy for postage & handling to:

Name: _____

Address: _____

City: _____ State: _____ Zip: _____

Enclosed is: ☐ check, ☐ M.O.

Allow 4 to 6 Weeks for delivery.

ETHIOPIAN COOKBOOK ENTERPRISES   ISBN 0-9616345-1-0
                                         Sug. Ret. $14.99

ETHIOPIAN COOKBOOK ENTERPRISES

3800 POWELL LANE, Suite 404
FALLS CHURCH, VA 22041

Please send _____ copies of Exotic Ethiopian Cooking at $14.99 plus $2.00 per copy for postage & handling to:

Name: _____

Address: _____

City: _____ State: _____ Zip: _____

Enclosed is: ☐ check, ☐ M.O.

Allow 4 to 6 Weeks for delivery.

ETHIOPIAN COOKBOOK ENTERPRISES   ISBN 0–9616345–1–0
Sug. Ret. $14.99